WOMEN'S CONFLICTS ABOUT EATING AND SEXUALITY: THE RELATIONSHIP BETWEEN FOOD AND SEX

Rosalyn M. Meadow, PhD
Lillie Weiss, PhD

SOME ADVANCE REVIEWS

"A provocative analysis of how our basic needs for food, sex, and love become confounded and confused. This clearly written and carefully researched book will help professionals understand patients with eating disorders as victims of destructive social pressures. It provides practical answers for every woman who is struggling to live in a body that seems constantly out of control."

Rita Freedman, PhD
Author, *Body-Love: Learning to Like Our Looks and Ourselves*;
Clinical Psychologist, Scarsdale, New York

"This book is unique . . . Drs. Meadow and Weiss reveal the interplay between food and sexuality, the beginnings of the women's movement, the sexual revolution, and the subsequent acceleration of eating disorders in our society. We learn why it is that women are shifting their focus from sexual to oral obsessions. . . . This unusual book shows us just how it is that sex and food satisfy female needs for love and dependency and thereby prepares us for a new phase in the emancipation of women. . . . A tour de force which no one who cares about the changing roles of women can afford to be without."

Violet Franks, PhD
Director of Clinical Services
Carrier Foundation
Belle Mead, New Jersey

Women's Conflicts About Eating and Sexuality

The Relationship Between Food and Sex

HAWORTH Women's Studies
Ellen Cole, PhD and Esther Rothblum, PhD
Senior Co-Editors

New, Recent, and Forthcoming Titles:

When Husbands Come Out of the Closet by Jean Schaar Gochros

Prisoners of Ritual: An Odyssey into Female Genital Circumcision in Africa by Hanny Lightfoot-Klein

Foundations for a Feminist Restructuring of the Academic Disciplines edited by Michele Paludi and Gertrude A. Steuernagel

Hippocrates' Handmaidens: Women Married to Physicians by Esther Nitzberg

Waiting: A Diary of Loss and Hope in Pregnancy by Ellen Judith Reich

God's Country: A Case Against Theocracy by Sandy Rapp

Women and Aging: Celebrating Ourselves by Ruth Raymond Thone

A Woman's Odyssey into Africa: Tracks Across a Life by Hanny Lightfoot-Klein

Women's Conflicts About Eating and Sexuality: The Relationship Between Food and Sex by Rosalyn M. Meadow and Lillie Weiss

Anorexia Nervosa and Recovery: A Hunger for Meaning by Karen Way

Reproductive Hazards in the Workplace: Mending Jobs, Managing Pregnancies by Regina Kenen

Women Murdered by the Men They Loved by Constance A. Bean

Women's Conflicts About Eating and Sexuality

The Relationship Between Food and Sex

Rosalyn M. Meadow, PhD
Lillie Weiss, PhD

The Haworth Press
New York • London • Norwood (Australia)

The Haworth Press, Inc., 10 Alice Street, Binghamton, NY 13904-1580

Library of Congress Cataloging-in-Publication Data

Meadow, Rosalyn M.
   Women's conflicts about eating and sexuality: the relationship between food and sex / Rosalyn M. Meadow, Lillie Weiss.
       p.   cm.
   Includes bibliographical references and index.
   ISBN 1-56024-131-4 (acid-free paper)
   1. Eating disorders—United States—History—20th century. 2. Psychosexual disorders—United States—History—20th century. 3. Women—Mental health—United States—History—20th century. I. Weiss, Lillie. II. Title.
RC552.E18M43 1992
616.85'260082—dc20   91-4120
                                                                                 CIP

CONTENTS

ABOUT THE AUTHORS

Rosalyn M. Meadow, PhD, and **Lillie Weiss, PhD**, are psychologists in private practice who each have over 20 years of experience working with women with eating disorders and sexual problems. They have collaborated on a variety of projects, including many papers and several narrated slide presentations. Drs. Meadow and Weiss have run numerous workshops and classes on sexuality and eating disorders, trained physicians and clinicians, and spoken at national and international conferences.

Dr. Meadow is a certified sex therapist, specializing in sexual dysfunctions. Previously, she was Professor of Sociology at Scottsdale Community College where she introduced Human Sexuality courses into the curriculum. In her doctoral dissertation, she examined the relationship between women's weight and their sexual responsiveness. Dr. Meadow is a member of the American Psychological Association.

Dr. Weiss is Director of the Clinical Psychology Center at Arizona State University. A member of the Arizona State Psychological Association and the Maricopa Psychological Society, she is the author of three books, including *Treating Bulimia: A Psychoeducational Approach* (Pergamon Press, 1985), and *You Can't Have Your Cake and Eat It Too: A Program for Controlling Bulimia* (R. & E. Publishers, 1986).

Preface

We wrote this book for every woman who steps on the scale with fear and trepidation, anxiously awaiting the verdict. It is a book for every woman who believes she is too fat and is never happy with her weight. It is a book for the young single woman who finds comfort from a soothing scoop of ice cream, the career woman who squeezes daily aerobic classes into her already busy schedule, and for all the women who know the caloric content of every morsel that crosses their lips.

The seeds for our book germinated several years ago as we were eating lunch and discussing the food madness pervading our culture. We noted that some women were starving themselves, others threw up their food or tortured their bodies through exercise, and some even submitted to surgery to be thin. Our lunchtime conversation extended into more conversation about the lengths to which women would go in their pursuit of thinness. As psychologists who have each worked with women for over 20 years, we wanted to understand this strange preoccupation with food. We knew that for a phenomenon to be so pervasive, it had to tap into a universal need for women. We felt that this was not a passing fad or fancy but an obsession that had at its core issues of major significance for women. We tried to *really* understand this strange state of affairs, not only on an intellectual level, but to get under women's skins and empathize with what was going on. We explored our own feelings, we listened to our clients, we talked to our friends, we read the popular and professional literature, and we observed the culture. Slowly we came to understand that food and eating were a metaphor for what is required for survival as a woman in today's society.

The more we explored this phenomenon, the more we could see a striking resemblance between the current conflict—to eat or not to eat—and the dilemma for women 30 years ago—to do "it" or not to do "it." Having grown up in the 1950s and 1960s ourselves and having seen hundreds of women in therapy who had to monitor their sexual behavior, we could see a startling similarity between today's eating problems and the sexual conflicts several decades ago. The symptoms have changed but the underlying dilemma remains the same. Women are still repressing their basic needs—whether they be oral or sexual—in order to be loved.

We wanted to share our observations and insights with other women and with men. We believe the issues we raise are relevant for any woman growing up in our society—and for her spouse, brother, father, or son. Most of our examples are about heterosexual, middle-class, white women because that is what we are familiar with. However, conflicts about eating are not limited to heterosexual women and apply to lesbians as well.

By writing this book, we hope that we women can free ourselves from the absurdities we have endorsed and help in creating a society that does not make our self-worth contingent on deprivation of our most basic of needs, a society where we can nourish ourselves at all levels. We have freed ourselves from our shackles in the past and we know we can do so again. The sexual revolution came about with much consciousness-raising and women challenging the myths about their sexuality. We believe that the time is ripe to overthrow the tyranny of thinness and the cultural demands for a perfect body.

We see this book as a revolutionary new book of the 1990s.

Chapter 1

Good Girls Don't Eat Dessert

"What's wrong with me? I feel awful. Just because I gained five pounds, I feel so bad about myself. I feel disgusting, ugly, and fat. I know a few pounds don't mean anything, but *why does my self-esteem depend on how much I weigh?*" As psychologists, we hear these words daily from our clients. Almost every woman we talk to worries about her weight and lets it affect her mood and the way she feels about herself. We recognize the irrationality of these statements, but as women, we can identify with the fear of being too fat. Although women have always worried about their weight, what we see today is an obsession that goes beyond mere worry. We are observing a phenomenon so pervasive that the 1980s have been labeled the decade of the eating disorders. Today's women are *obsessed* with their weight. They are preoccupied with dieting, exercise, and becoming thin.

In our practices, we see women who starve themselves, throw up their food, and abuse their bodies to be slim. More and more women are resorting to surgery in their pursuit of thinness. Roughly two million young women suffer from anorexia or bulimia, and countless numbers binge periodically on junk food. Startling research results show that two out of five single women go through periods of binge eating, and one out of three women diets *once a month.* Diet foods, diet pills, diet clinics, diet books...a diet mentality pervades the country. Millions and millions of dollars are spent by women pursuing a thin body.

Women torment themselves with thoughts of forbidden foods and do not allow themselves to act on their natural desire to eat. They count every calorie that passes their lips, and they live in a constant state of deprivation and hunger. They fear going out of control by becoming fat and ruining their chances for love and career, because being thin in our society is equated with being successful, competent, and lovable. Women are afraid that their chances for love and

1

career success will be diminished if they do not meet the current standard of bodily perfection.

Food has become a source of incredible anxiety for millions of women, simultaneously being an object of dread and of intense desire. Women are engaged in an ongoing battle with food: craving it, fearing it, and letting it control their lives. The battle between abstinence and indulgence is waged on a daily basis. As one woman put it, "It's like the Thirty Years War, only more personal," (Marks, 1988). She describes the turmoil generated by conflict:

> Why has this ordinary thing, eating, become the motor driving my life? I walk down the street as though it's a minefield, with the mines being the fast-food shops and their intoxicating aromas beckoning me to blow up my resolve. I know they are dangerous, but they're also heady and seductive—like the call of the Lorelei...should I wear a clothespin when I take a walk? Blinders? A muzzle?

The constant fight to contain the bodily hungers requires a superhuman effort, particularly where there is so much emphasis on gourmet delights everywhere one turns. Watching a food commercial on television and not eating is like watching a pornographic film and abstaining. Women wrestle with this dilemma daily, desire alternating with denial.

The extreme case is the anorexic who goes through the agony of suppressing drives so strong that they require constant vigilance. The more she feels her needs, the more she crushes them, to the point that, at times, her behavior becomes life-threatening. Many women rebel against the deprivation with uncontrollable outbursts of food binges. They let their passion run rampant and later feel guilt and remorse for their shameful, compulsive behavior. They vow they will never let their passion get out of control again and lash themselves for their weakness. This "lashing" often transcends mental flagellation and becomes the physical act of purging—a sign of bulimia— accomplished by vomiting or taking laxatives to get rid of the food they have ingested. Post-binge periods of starvation and fanatical exercise are also methods of purging. For many compulsive eaters, their desire is so great that it cannot be curbed, in spite of societal pressure and even health risks.

These behaviors are extreme, of course, representing women with known eating disorders, but unfortunately, they are not so different from the behaviors of "normal" women in their daily battle with food. How many of us women—except those lucky few with active metabolisms—have not experienced pangs of guilt after indulging in a hot fudge sundae? How many of us can honestly say that we can enjoy a meal without any awareness or consciousness of calorie content? How many women do not worry about getting fat? "Have I eaten too much? Have I gone too far?" we ask ourselves. "How much can I eat without crossing the line, the line between fat and thin?"

It is almost impossible to be a woman in this culture without having engaged in the war against food. Each woman has her own battle plan. Some women only fill their grocery carts with fruits and vegetables, while others have permanently written off sugar and white flour. Many women will not put anything into their mouths after 6:00 p.m., whereas some diet stringently during the week and let themselves go on weekends. A large number of women only permit themselves dessert if it is Weight Watchers', and an even larger number keep a daily running tab of the amount of calories they consume. There are those women who do not eat anything all day long but allow themselves to have dinner; and then there are those who eat whatever they like but exercise every day. Some women weigh themselves daily and fast when the scale goes beyond a certain point, and some fast every other day.

For every act of self-denial, there is one of self-indulgence, one where the urges of the body go unabashedly rampant. There are those women whose first thoughts upon awakening, and last thoughts before going to sleep, are of food; those who devour ice cream in gallons; those who hide candy bars and cram them down their throats when nobody is looking; those who drive in a frenzy from store to store in the middle of the night in search for food. There are career women who cannot wait till they come home from work so that they can binge, and there are housewives who raid the refrigerator after everyone has gone to sleep. There are even women who refuse dates so they can stay home and eat, and there are some women who derive more passion from a Mars bar than a sexual encounter. Women are caught up in a whirlwind in their desire for food. They are obsessed ...obsessed...obsessed. For countless women, their lust has reached such proportions that food has become their lover.

The love-hate relationship with food is a major source of conflict for many women. Thousands of women approach each day wondering whether it will be a good or a bad day—all depending on the numbers on their scale. They are preoccupied with what they will eat, how much, and whether they can permit themselves to abstain. They fantasize about food, dream about it, and yet do not allow themselves to act on their desires. They use food to soothe themselves if they are upset, to calm themselves if they are angry, and to comfort themselves if they are sad. Food has become a metaphor for their emotions.

Our culture only reinforces this craziness for food with its double messages. For every diet commercial, there is a fast-food commercial, and for every image of a slim body, there is an equally alluring image of a gourmet dish. For every weight loss article, there is a mouth-watering recipe, perpetuating the conflict with food. Should I or should I not indulge? Do I dare cross that line, that line between thin and fat, good and bad? Do I dare give in to my impulses?

As psychologists who have worked with women for over two decades, we wanted to understand this strange state of affairs, this food madness. We asked ourselves what basic underlying fear would motivate such extreme behavior. We wondered why women would take such extraordinary measures to deny their basic needs and why a few extra pounds on their hips would strike such terror in their hearts. We spent hours in discussion trying to comprehend why women were engaging in such self-defeating behavior, and we saw a striking similarity between women's eating concerns today and their concerns about their sexuality in the past. We recognized a parallel between the major conflict for women today—to eat or not to eat— and the old sexual conflict—to "do it" or not to "do it." Having grown up in the 1950s ourselves and having counseled hundreds of women who suffered the consequences of repressed sexuality, we could see a startling resemblance between current problems over food and eating and the sexual conflicts of yesteryear.

Years ago, women had the same feelings of guilt, trepidation, and fear about sex that they do today about food. To "do it" or not to "do it": that was the dilemma faced by women before the sexual revolution. They wrestled with this problem each time they went out on a date and tormented themselves with worry about "going all the way." They dreamed and fantasized about letting go and succumbing to the waves of desire. Images of sexual ecstasy alternated with feelings of terror lest they become pregnant and ruined for life. Good girls learned to repress their sexual appetites because the consequences of having intercourse could be severe. A young woman had to remain a good girl at all costs; that is, she did everything possible to keep her hymen intact for her wedding night. If she had sex before marriage, she was considered damaged goods and risked getting a reputation as being easy.

Good girls were the kind men respected and married, the kind that men brought home to Mother. They were clean and pure, in contrast to the bad girls who everyone knew were doing it. Bad girls were for fun but not for marriage, and with one slip, a good girl could easily find herself talked about, whispered about, ostracized and unsuitable for marriage. Without a husband, a woman was nothing: a man promised her an identity as well as financial security. Unmarried women were viewed with disdain, as second-class citizens doomed to live with their parents. No woman in her right mind wanted to become an old maid; every woman wanted an MRS degree because she received her status and her worth from her husband and children.

To be marriageable, a woman had to vigilantly monitor her sexual desires since her whole future depended on how well she kept her sexual impulses in check. The fear of being labeled a "bad girl" and not getting married was constantly in the back of her mind, just as the fear of becoming fat predominates women's thoughts today. Going out of control may mean losing it all.

An out-of-wedlock pregnancy was the ultimate shame and humiliation and reinforced women's suppression of their natural sexual impulses, just as the fear of an obese frame serves to keep women's appetites in check today. Unmarried girls who became pregnant were hidden away out of town, either with relatives or in special homes for unwed mothers, much in the same way that many obese women resort to self-imposed hiding when their shame becomes too much to bear. The disgrace of going out of control sexually was so great that some women risked death through back-alley butchers who performed illegal abortions. When we read stories today about women risking death through liposuction or intestinal bypass surgery, we are reminded of the horror stories we heard years ago about botched abortions. We are saddened by the desperation that drives women to these drastic measures.

In spite of the dreaded consequences of losing control sexually, women continued to fantasize about the pleasures of the forbidden fruit, dreaming about giving in to their passions and experiencing the ultimate in ecstasy. Because sex carried with it elements of mystery and intrigue, it became very enticing and uppermost in women's thoughts. Sexual fantasies fueled the imagination, and women became obsessed with having sexual intercourse. Sex was fraught with danger and excitement and was always on women's minds, so that they could hardly wait for the day when they could come together with their lovers. Romance magazines, novels, and movies portrayed sex as passionate and glorious, serving to keep the obsession with sex alive in women's imaginations. Today, food advertisements in print and on television tantalize women and fuel their consuming passions for forbidden foods.

The agony and the ecstasy of succumbing to the passions of the flesh were ever-present in women's imaginations. Sex was at once the ultimate danger and the ultimate delight, creating a continuous struggle between experiencing sexual pleasure and risking their future. The paradox for those women was that to be loved by a man, they had to deny themselves the most basic way of experiencing love: they had to deprive themselves of their natural, instinctual sexual appetites.

The constant repression of normal bodily drives resulted in a variety of sexual disorders in women, including the inability to achieve orgasm and complete lack of sexual desire. Seven out of ten women could not experience sexual satisfaction consistently and were often frustrated. Many others could not even get aroused and had to seek psychiatric treatment for their inhibited sexual desires (ISD). Like anorexia, inhibited sexual desire is a disorder of the appetite. The woman is devoid of erotic feelings and receives no pleasure from sexual activity. Like the anorexic who turns herself off from food, the sexual anorexic has shut off her erotic feelings. In both illnesses, the issue of control is at the center. The fear of loss of control and suffering the abhorrent consequences is so great that these women have tried to stifle their bodily hungers by rising above them and denying they exist. Deprivation and starvation are at the core of these disorders.

Another consequence of constant sexual repression was a form of sexual bulimia for some women. The sexual bulimic alternated between episodes of being a good girl or being bad. Her periods of sexual starvation usually followed sexual acting out. Her one-night stands can be compared to binging behavior, resulting in shame and repulsion and a strong commitment to never let this happen again. She vowed time and time again not to let her bodily hungers control her, but regardless of how hard she tried, she succumbed to them over and over. Like the bulimic, the sexual bulimic purged herself of her sins—with a "morning after" pill rather than a laxative.

Not all women experienced sexual disorders, of course, but every woman was faced with some form of the basic conflict—to do it or not to do it. How could she satisfy her normal bodily desires without risking the severe consequences? The sexual revolution liberated women from this conflict and gave them permission to exercise their sexual rights by encouraging them to experiment sexually and free themselves from their inhibitions. However, old patterns of repression were hard to break, and a large number of women could not enjoy their newfound freedom. Women had learned to control their erotic impulses so well that many could not let go and experience orgasm.

As psychotherapists, we saw hundreds of women who were attempting to free themselves from their sexual shackles. Because they were kept in the dark for so long, getting their information primarily from whispers and romantic novels, women needed to learn about the physiological aspects of sex. We conducted groups and seminars to teach them about their bodies and to correct many of the romantic myths that they had been fed.

As a result of the sexual revolution, there has been a vast shift in the attitudes toward female sexuality in that we are neither expected to repress our sexual desires nor do we have to remain virgins to be loved. No longer are large numbers of women knocking on our doors because of conflicts about their sexual behavior; now women come to us with different problems.

In our practices, we are witnessing the new "Good Girls Don't" phenomenon revolving around eating and dieting—a shift in women's central preoccupation from sex to food. In fact, there is a declining interest in sexual activity. Now we see women who have little or no erotic desire; women who want us to teach them to enhance their appetite for sex and to control their appetite for food. The major conflict has become: to eat or not to eat.

The guilt generated by this conflict is heard in comments such as these:

> I always lie about my weight. I don't want anyone to know how much I weigh. That's because I'm ashamed of it. I hate my fat hips and thighs. They're grotesque. I feel like everyone's thinner than I am. They always look good, and I am a fat, disgusting thing. But I don't really do anything about it. Oh, I try to be good, but I always fail. When I have dinner, I just can't stop eating. It's a lost cause. I hate being size 12.

Women who voice this despair are obsessed about food in the same way their mothers used to be obsessed about sex, their thoughts alternating between passion and guilt. Just as women once described themselves as good girls when they had exercised control over their bodies by not succumbing to the demands of the flesh, women today castigate themselves for not being good because they let their appetites get the best of them. They hate themselves for being weak, expressing a great deal of self-loathing and disgust.

The fat woman is today's equivalent of yesterday's bad girl. Her body announces to the world that she has let her desires run rampant, and she is ostracized just as though she had an "A" for *Adultress* emblazoned on her chest. The consequences of becoming obese can be just as traumatic for women as the consequences of being sexually active had been in the past. The fat woman fears that she will find nobody to love her if she lets herself act on her oral appetite. For this reason, many of us continue to deny our basic hungers.

At the same time that food can provide so much pleasure and

satisfaction, it can also be a source of conflict. Statements such as these, made by average-weight women, are common and indicative of the extent to which eating is conflict-ridden:

> Whenever I'm depressed, I come home, have a hot shower and get into bed with my Three Musketeers. I concentrate on each mouthful, chewing slowly and absorbing the chocolaty sensation. When I'm finished, I feel better and then read for a while. The next morning I am consumed with guilt.

What a shame that we cannot allow ourselves the pleasures of eating without feeling guilt and remorse! Why should we feel so bad and conflict-ridden about gaining a few pounds? The reason for our agony is that we are afraid—afraid that nobody will love us if we are fat.

Another average-weight woman's comment illustrates how the soothing capacity of food sometimes depends not only on *what* is eaten, but also on *how much* is eaten.

> Frequently, I like to get into bed with a bag of Oreos and a good book. It's one of my favorite things to do, and I just love it. But then when I weigh myself the next day, I feel terrible.

She gets into bed, not with a handful of Oreos, but with a whole bag, telling herself, in effect, "I'm so needy (i.e., stressed out, overworked, lonely, etc.) that I deserve a whole bag," and then reprimanding herself for succumbing to her need and her self-pity. Often women admit that their reason for eating an entire bag, box, or carton of "no-no" foods is to conceal from their mate how much they have eaten: if they eat three-quarters of a box of cookies, the mostly empty box will remain in the cupboard as evidence that they have binged—evidence that could be discovered by their mate. If, on the other hand, they can throw away the empty package, they need not fear discovery. Some women even go so far as to rush to the store and buy a replacement for the missing box, if its absence will be noticed by their man. We know one woman who would frequently eat a whole box of Wheat Thins, and though her husband never touched those crackers, she would leave the empty box on the shelf for a week or so, just to maintain the appearance of the crackers' presence—and her self-control.

The conflict over food goes beyond eating—it goes to the essence of a woman's being: who will love me if I'm fat? Another aspect of this conflict strikes at her sex-role identity: what should I be, mother or career woman? How can I be both and still be loved? Food and thinness are only symbols of this conflict. Slimness symbolizes a rejection of the matronly figure and an espousal of the image of achievement. Today we are being told that we can do it all, that we can perform equally in the bedroom and the boardroom. Thinness has become equated with women's quest for perfection: that she can be disciplined and successful like a man, and beautiful and desirable like a woman.

Just as thinness is a symbol, so too are food and hunger metaphors for deeper emotional expressions: they are manifestations of intensely felt emotional experiences. Food represents the most primitive form of love and nurturing, in that receiving milk from the breast is the infant's first loving encounter and fusion with another human being. When the baby hungers for nourishment, it is longing for more than just the taste of the milk. When we talk about women's conflicts with food, we are not merely discussing physical drives and taste buds. We are talking about an emotional hunger and the need to be loved. More than that, we are talking about *denial* of needs, a denial that is being expressed through starvation in the midst of plenty.

Unfortunately, the paradox is that in order to be loved, a woman believes that she must deny her most basic needs. To receive emotional nourishment, she feels she has to deprive herself of her bodily nourishment, sometimes at the risk of her health and safety. We women are still reaching for a standard of lovability, whether it be in the form of an intact hymen or a size six dress. We are still seeking approval from men, and we are *still trying to be good girls*. In spite of her navy blue business suit and assertive rhetoric, today's woman is still suppressing her needs in order to conform to society's standards of acceptance and lovability.

We asked ourselves what basic underlying fear would motivate this extreme behavior. We wondered why women would take such extraordinary measures to deny their instinctual needs for food and sex to conform to the cultural norms of acceptability and to remain good girls at all costs. When we looked at the parallels between sexual and oral repression, we observed that the way women defined themselves had not changed. Although the women's movement enabled us to have careers, at bottom, the psychology of women remained the same. Women's central focus in life has always been the quest for an ideal love relationship. When we find a man who loves us, we feel unique, important, and special. A man's love is the proof that a woman is valuable and cherished. Although the feminists argued that women could attain value, importance, and security through achievement, a woman still seeks her identity through a relationship with a man. The cultural heroine is still the bride and not the corporate executive. Thus, we concluded that women's needs for attachment, connectedness, and belonging are so powerful that they are willing to thwart their life-supporting drives to adapt to society's criteria of lovability. Despite all the social progress of the last thirty years, women will still do anything for love.

The struggle to meet our basic needs and become our own person while, at the same time, finding someone to love us has always faced women. Why is this universal conflict between dependence and self-expression manifesting itself through food today? Why have we shifted our focus from sexual to oral obsessions? Why do we turn to food rather than to sex for comfort? What part does the culture play in this world of inhibited sexual desire and increased eating disorders? Why are good girls still denying themselves dessert?

In the following pages, we examine the role that food and sex have played in women's lives. We compare the conflict—to eat or not to eat—to the major conflict for women thirty years ago—to do it or not to do it. We spell out the parallels between sex and eating, and their relationships to women's basic need to be loved. Food, sex and love are areas of vital concern to every woman, from the adolescent who diets to the grandmother who joins an aerobics class. Our book is for every woman who has agonized over whether or not to eat a chocolate ice cream cone. It is for every woman who feels fear and trepidation before stepping on the scales. It is for every woman who has ever worried that she was too fat or too sexual. It is for every woman who is afraid of indulging herself lest she lose love, and for every woman who indulges because she lacks love.

By writing this book, we hope to make other women aware of current cultural influences on their thoughts and behavior. We hope they will see themselves in these pages, and will examine and question their behavior so that they can learn to change it. We believe that as women, we can learn to meet our need for love without denying our natural instincts.

The combined efforts of the women's movement and the sexual revolution brought awareness to millions of women about how they had repressed themselves sexually. They questioned the arbitrary sexual restrictions imposed on them by society and challenged them. When they banded together and allowed themselves sexual expression, they discovered that there were not dire consequences: they could still be loved—with or without a hymen. When they freed themselves from their sexual restraints, they also freed themselves from much unnecessary guilt, worry, and conflict.

It is our fervent hope that women can challenge the arbitrary societal norms of thinness and bodily perfection that are contributing to so much guilt, shame, and self-loathing. It is time for us to set ourselves free from hunger, deprivation, and bodily abuses. It is time for a new revolution!

Chapter 2

The Love Affair with Food

It's just that I'm into nutrition, and I have to get away from sex.

— "Mayflower Madam" Sydney Biddle Barrows, on why she would like to write an advice column on nutrition and "interpersonal relationships."
From the *New York Post.*

Women today are simultaneously—and paradoxically—obsessed with food and bodily perfection. Diet and exercise are our main topics of conversation. We juggle our already busy schedules to fit aerobics classes into our daily lives, even as our fascination grows with food and its preparation. Gourmet shops, cookbooks, and trendy restaurants have increasing popularity, and exotic foods are now the objects of women's fantasies. At the same time, there is a decreasing interest in sex, with lack of desire being the number one sexual problem among women today. We no longer put our main emphasis on sex and romance; we no longer daydream about the mysterious, forbidden, and romantic sexual encounter. Now we daydream about that bag of potato chips "calling our name" from the cupboard; now the obsessive focus is on food.

Of paramount concern to women today are the issues of when to eat, how much to eat, and what to eat. Women want to be thin at all costs because in today's world being thin is equated with being loveable, desirable, and successful. The underlying fear is that if we let ourselves become fat, we will never find a man to love us, or the man we love might leave us. Dieting has become a symbolic expression of the lengths to which we will go to achieve lovability.

In the absence of love, food provides a comforting substitute for erotic pleasure, particularly in this age of career pressures, conflicting sex roles, and insecurity in relationships. Food can fill the emptiness and feelings of loneliness created in this pressure-filled world. Food makes no demands, is readily available, and provides instant gratification. It is more than a physical nourishment; it is emotional nourishment as well. Food has become a lover. Yet women must give up this lover to find love; this is their conflict.

Women of all ages are plagued by this conflict, from the girl in grade school to the grandmother going to Weight Watchers. (We have read about aerobics classes as the theme for little girls' birthday parties!) How can we resolve the seemingly unsolvable dilemma of physically and emotionally nourishing ourselves and remaining slim at the same time? The fear of getting fat is illustrated in the following statements from our patients:

> If I don't exercise every day, I get scared because I'll get fatter and fatter.

> When I think about getting fat, I think about my mother, and I think about being ugly and non-sexual. When I'm thin, I feel sexy and attractive. I look at men, and they look at me. I flirt and feel young and sexy. When I get fat, I feel old and matronly. Now I'm ten pounds overweight and hate it. I want to hide instead of talking to men and teasing with them.

Women are terrified of losing control. They fear they will balloon out and nobody will want them. The anxiety plagues them, and they castigate themselves for their weakness. The self-loathing when they cannot keep their passions in check is aptly illustrated in the next statement:

> I hate myself when I get fat. It's sick. My stomach gets big, and it disgusts me. Then I yell at myself, "How could you have let that happen?"

The most startling thing about these statements is that they are made by women who are not fat and who do not have eating disorders. These are average women who do not allow themselves to enjoy the pleasures of eating without feeling guilty. The self-hatred is plain to see. Women feel ashamed of their lack of control and beat themselves over the head if they gain a few pounds. Their happiness and state of mind are contingent on numbers: on the scale, on their clothing tags, and in their daily calorie counts.

CATHY: "I JUST CAN'T CONTROL MY EATING"

In our practice, we see many women whose preoccupations with food have become uncontrollable obsessions. These women are forever fantasizing about what they are going to eat next, constantly daydreaming about their next meal. Cathy is an example of such a woman whose appetite for food appears to be insatiable, although one would not know it by looking at her svelte, trim figure. Cathy, in her designer clothes and sophisticated hairstyle and make-up, looks the image of the successful career woman she happens to be. She displays a smooth, confident exterior as she talks, gesturing at times with her long, immaculately manicured nails.

"I wasn't always like this," she begins, as she describes her obsession with food. "Many years ago, I was a young happy housewife, raising my two girls, and thinking I had the perfect marriage. Then— bam—one day, out of a clear blue sky, my husband left me for another woman, and there I was, young, uneducated, totally alone, with two young girls. I cried, and I felt sorry for myself, and I did all the things you do when your world is falling apart. Then, one day, I decided to go on a diet and to exercise. I was never really heavy, and I never had a problem with food, but I thought maybe if I did something for myself I would feel better. As I lost weight, I started to get male attention. So I began to drive myself harder and to exercise more. I would run, oh, one to two hours a day, and then I'd feel really good. But it seemed to me that I was not getting much thinner, so I would starve myself and restrict myself until I would literally be hallucinating about food.

"One day I couldn't control myself any longer. I went on my first real binge. I remember walking into the supermarket, heading directly for the cookies and junk foods and walking away with several bags of cookies, potato chips, ice cream—you name it. I didn't even wait to get home. I sat in my car and devoured everything until I couldn't even taste it any more. My stomach was so hard it felt like it was going to burst. My head was swimming, and I don't know how I managed to drive home. I barely made it to the bathroom, where I got sick to my stomach and threw up all that I had eaten. I was so weak afterwards that I could barely walk. I remember having an awful headache and feeling so embarrassed and disgusted with myself. But when I got on the scale the next day, I was elated that I still weighed the same. I recall thinking to myself that I don't have to starve myself any more. I can eat whatever I want and still be thin.

"That was the beginning of the binging. I used to binge about once a week. Then it gradually increased to the point where I would do this every day. If I was at home and not working, I would binge and throw up several times a day. A few times I tried to stop the crazy behavior, but it was out of my control. Around this time, I also got a job as an airline stewardess and had to be weighed all the time to meet their requirements. That just seemed to feed into what I was doing to myself. Now I am obsessed with food. All I can think of day and night is what I am going to eat next. Visions of cookies and chocolate eclairs appear in front of me as I am trying to do my work, as I talk to people. No matter what I am doing, I am always planning my next binge.

"Two years ago I got a new job. I also met a wonderful man. We started seeing each other regularly and fell in love to the point that we decided to get married. At that time I thought to myself, 'Well, now you have it all again, you don't need to binge all the time any more.' " At this point, Cathy's calm exterior started to disintegrate as she let out the tears. "I really thought that if everything went okay in my life again, I would stop being so obsessed with food. But I still am, and I can't understand it. Tom and I got married two weeks ago. We went on this wonderful romantic honeymoon, and even while we were making love, all I could think of was when would we stop so that I could eat. While he was touching me, all I could picture were images of food. I am so obsessed with it, I don't know what to do. I've heard it said men lust for women, and women lust for food. I never realized how true that was—or how pathetic."

FOOD: THE CONSUMING PASSION

Cathy's obsession with food appears quite extreme; however, her story is echoed in varying degrees by women of all ages and all walks of life—high school and college students, career women, housewives, mothers and grandmothers. Some display their obsession openly, and their obese frames declare their uncontrollable addiction to food. Others, like Cathy, have learned ways to keep their preoccupation hidden from others. Fasting, laxative use, vomiting, and excessive exercise—these are all ways of keeping others from discovering their shameful secret. These women have been termed *bulimics,* or *binge-purgers.*

However, there are some nonbulimic women who think about food all the time even though they do not binge. There are women whose eating patterns resemble scaled-down binging. These women will eat large portions of food and will find it very difficult to stop eating once they start. These women are *compulsive overeaters*, and this intense preoccupation with food is termed an *obsession.*

When a woman is obsessed with food, she makes it the focus of her existence. It is as though she cannot think about anything else: Her whole life appears to revolve around the object of the obsession. From her first waking moment, she thinks about what she will have for breakfast or whether she will skip it that morning. She plans exactly what she is going to eat that day, how many calories she will allow herself and how she can keep herself from losing control. As the morning goes on, she constantly looks at the clock, waiting for lunchtime and fantasizing about what she will eat. She imagines the different foods and tries not to think about them. She will be good...she will be good, she vows. At lunchtime, she only orders a salad while looking wistfully at the rich hamburgers, french fries, and creamy desserts being consumed by other restaurant patrons. She only allows herself a teaspoon of dressing and carefully watches everything she puts into her mouth. She feels deprived and can only focus on food. It is difficult for her to concentrate on the conversation of others as she tries to make the salad last as long as possible. She hungers for that slice of warm, crusty, freshly baked French bread, but she denies herself the pleasure. And that is all she can think about as the lunch hour progresses.

As the afternoon wears on, her thoughts about food become more intense and more frequent. She tries to make the images go away, but they don't. She can almost taste the hot, buttered bread. The longing becomes deeper, more and more intense. By the time she leaves work, there is only one thought on her mind: FOOD. She cannot think about anything else. She thinks about the skinless chicken breast and frozen string beans waiting for her at home, and the hour it would take to cook her meal. She cannot wait. Images of succulent fried chicken keep intruding as she sees the Kentucky Fried Chicken sign. I will only get one piece, she tells herself. I will take the skin off.

She drives madly to Kentucky Fried Chicken, and before she can control herself, she orders a whole bucket of chicken, rolls, and mashed potatoes in gravy. It doesn't matter that these contain millions of calories; it doesn't matter that she was good all day; it doesn't matter what she will look like at the beach. Nothing matters except wanting to eat that chicken. She is blind to everything else.

There is almost a desperation as she races home, opening the bucket of chicken as soon as she is inside the door. She eats and eats and eats, as though she can never get enough. Depriving herself at breakfast and lunch certainly contributed to her feelings, but a hungry person would have stopped once hunger was satisfied. This is more than hunger.

Although consuming a whole bucket of chicken may be an extreme manifestation of obsessive behavior, the constant dwelling on food, calories, and dieting is commonplace today. "Normal" women of all ages and sizes are preoccupied by food. They talk about it, think about it, daydream about it, and read about it. They look at cookbooks, diet books, compare recipes, and discuss restaurants that serve low calorie foods. They buy books that tell them to the utmost degree the caloric content of each morsel that passes their lips. When they go to the supermarket, they buy diet sodas and Lean Cuisine and studiously examine and compare caloric contents of different products.

Paradoxically, women alternate between depriving themselves and talking about the last delicious meal they had. Frequently, when women go out for lunch, they will have an animated conversation about the latest gourmet shops and restaurants as they nibble on a leafy green salad with low calorie dressing and sip sugarless iced tea. Their behavior resembles that of the anorexic who loves to talk about food. They will rave about the newest bakery and excitedly describe the mouth-watering desserts. But when the waiter strolls over with the dessert tray, they will quickly say, "No thanks, just coffee for me," then glance longingly and surreptitiously—so the companions will not notice—at the chocolate cake as it is carried away. They must maintain their image of self-control even around other women because they seek approval and validation from them as well as men, but even more so because they are in competition with each other, battling for love.

There is a passionate longing for the delights of the forbidden, but like the good girls that they are, they stick to their spartan regimens and deny temptation much like the good girls of yesteryear, who deprived themselves sexually while engaging in secret, animated conversations about the forbidden pleasures of the flesh. The focus of the obsessive behavior has changed over the years, but the underlying conflict remains the same. Good girls are still depriving themselves of their basic needs to meet the criteria of "lovability," be it an intact hymen or a size 6 figure. Through the generations, women's behavioral patterns have remained consistent because the fear of being alone and unloved is so overwhelming that they are willing to do almost anything for love. They have engaged in self-defeating, self-denying behaviors to meet their most basic needs for affiliation and relationships.

THE SEXUALIZATION OF FOOD: THE EATING ORGY

"I had the most ecstatic experience at dinner the other night," gushed Paula. "I was hungry all day and couldn't wait to finish my work so that I could go out and eat. I kept fantasizing where I would go and could almost taste the food. I decided to go to a wonderful Italian restaurant all by myself and have Fettucini Alfredo. The first bite was heavenly. I just let it sit in my mouth as I took in the sensations. It was wonderful, almost like I was having an orgasm."

"I love chocolate," said Maria, "especially chocolate ice cream. I will take a carton of my favorite chocolate ice cream to bed with me and crawl under the covers and dip my spoon in the carton. I wait until it becomes soft and smooth, just the right texture, before I devour it. Chocolate ice cream is not something I like. It is something I love, like having an affair. I do it secretly and in bed."

"I'm a chocoholic. I *love* chocolate—chocolate ice cream; chocolate mousse; chocolate truffles; rich, dark, imported candy bars. No matter how hard I try, I can't resist it. Sometimes I resolve not to eat chocolate for a week, but my resolve goes out the window if a chocolate dessert is put in front of me. Try as I may, once I start eating, there is no stopping. The desire becomes so strong, I lose control and keep eating until it's all gone."

"Chocolate goes very well with sex: before, during, after—it doesn't matter," says Helen Gurley Brown, according to Mira Stout (*Vanity Fair*, Feb. 1986). Stout states that chocolate is "sin, love, and luxury rolled into three bite-size syllables." She compares the melt-in-the-mouth statements about chocolate to falling in love, and presents the theory that phenylethymine, a natural ingredient in chocolate, simulates the hormonal effects of being in love.

The erotic qualities of food are displayed in newspapers and magazines, and advertising agencies use sexual terms when describing food products to excite and arouse the consumer. *The New York Times Book Review* recently ran an ad for Christopher Idone's book *Glorious American Food*, touting it as "the most beautiful, most original, most sensually gratifying book ever to be published on American food." The *Phoenix Gazette* (Sept. 1990) describes a "Better than Sex Cake."

Food and eating, when sexualized, are endowed not only with the power to arouse, but with a moral power as well. The article titled "Sweet Surrender: Sugar's Not the Bad Guy You Think It Is" (Lowe, 1988) implies a giving in to naughty, sweet abandon, even personifying sugar as a not-so-bad "guy" to give in to. Eroticized food is seen as sinful. The food section of the November 1985 issue of *Cosmopolitan* magazine presented two all-time Cosmo-girl favorites: "sinfully rich" chocolate cake labeled "the Bad," and a salad nicoise labeled "the Beautiful" (Sadowsky). Eating this sexualized food is fraught with excitement and danger.

Binging, like masturbation, is an activity done in secret that promotes a great deal of guilt and implies the need for punishment. Just as women used to label themselves based on their sexual behavior as "good" girls or "bad" girls, they now say, "I was bad" when they overeat. They describe themselves as "good" girls when they have been pure and have not indulged in fattening foods. They want to be good at all costs because the consequences of being a bad girl can be devastating: nobody will love them if they are bad. The bulimic is like the little girl in the nursery rhyme "who had a little curl right in the middle of her forehead. And when she was good, she was very, very good, but when she was bad, she was horrid."

JANE: THE VERY GOOD GIRL

The anorexic woman is a *very* good girl, in that she overcomes the desires of her body through denial. Jane was better than good: she was perfect. Jane's mother described her as her pride and joy. "I have never had any trouble with Jane," her mother stated. "She always did what her father and I told her to do. I honestly cannot remember a time when I have had to discipline her. We always had glowing reports from her teachers, and she never gave anyone any trouble. She was such a pretty little girl and so neat. She kept her room clean, and I never had to remind her to pick up after herself. Now I don't recognize her anymore, and it scares me to look at her. She is so pitifully thin that I fear she is wasting away to nothing. She used to have such beautiful dark curly hair and clear white skin. Now I feel like crying every time I look at her because her hair is dull, her skin has no color, and her bones stick out."

Jane was not always so skinny. Up until the age of 14, four years ago, she looked like any normal girl. One day her boyfriend told her she was too fat, and on her fourteenth birthday, Jane made a resolution that she was not going to eat any sweets for a whole year. Jane was very good about keeping her word, so good that she denied herself anything that had sugar in it. As she began to read the labels on food products, she deleted more and more foods from her diet. She delighted in the control she was gaining over her body and enjoyed her feelings of triumph and accomplishment. What had started out as a desire to lose weight quickly turned into an all-consuming obsession. Jane became assiduously studious in her choice of food, analyzing every morsel before putting it into her mouth. Her obsession with slimness extended to other behaviors: she started to exercise, doing sit-ups and push-ups, running, and going to aerobics classes. It was not unusual for her to spend three, four or even five hours a day stretching the limits of her body.

Jane does not experience hunger pangs any more. She had experienced them at the beginning, but constant denial has resulted in obliviousness to the messages of her body. Jane is also oblivious to feelings of fatigue in spite of the strenuous and excessive exercise. Her whole life revolves around food, and she thinks about it all the time. She visualizes all the wonderful foods that are available, fantasizing about them in detail, but since she does not allow herself to act on her fantasies, she becomes obsessed with the preparation of food and with feeding others. At dinner time, she watches everyone eat, encouraging her sisters to take second helpings. By doing this, she vicariously experiences the satisfaction of eating and avoids the temptation to eat by giving the food to others. In her spare time, she reads cookbooks and clips recipes from magazines. Her conversation is sprinkled with food references and detailed accounts of what she puts into her mouth.

Unlike Cathy, who acted on her food fantasies and then purged herself, Jane denied her lust for food. Cathy cleansed herself after her food orgies; Jane remained pure. She used self-control, determination and will power to fight the longings in her body. Jane's attempts to control the newly awakened stirrings of her body are reminiscent of the adolescent's fight to overcome her budding sexuality. She is theatened by her sexual feelings and pushes them aside. She is terrified of the dangers of the excesses of the body and staves off her desires. By denying her passions, she remains the "good girl."

FRAN: THE BIG BAD GIRL

The obese woman is a very bad girl, wearing her badness like a badge. Anyone looking at her can see that she has sinned by overindulging her passions. Her longings have been satisfied many times over, and she appears to be insatiable. She is a reflection of desire run rampant. Fran is so fat her doctor has told her that if she does not lose weight she will die. Fran is so fat that she cannot sit in the waiting room chair. Her arms are so large they are the size of an average woman's thigh. What remains of a pretty face is distorted by bloatedness. Her eyes are like slits peering out from her swollen, misshapen face. Fran looks much older than her 27 years.

"I was always heavy," she starts, "even as a child, but never this fat. I didn't get so fat until a few years ago when I stayed home to take care of my baby. All I did was eat, and I gained over a hundred pounds in less than three years. I was very bored at home, and my husband was working long hours. I had no car and was trapped at home. Food was my only entertainment. I literally ate all day long, from the time I woke up until the time I went to sleep. The only time I could get out of the house was to go to the grocery store where I would fill up my cart with potato chips, Doritos, cookies, ice cream, doughnuts, and whatever else looked good. Once in a while my husband would make a remark that I was getting too fat, but he didn't seem to mind very much, and it really didn't matter because we never went out anywhere, anyway.

"When my baby was three years old, I went to my doctor for my regular check-up. He was shocked by how much weight I had put on and told me that I had morbid obesity and that I would die if I didn't lose weight. He scared me so much I followed his advice, went to Weight Watchers, and lost about seventy pounds. While I was losing weight, I met a man and had an affair. I began to think about divorcing my husband, and I found myself looking at men all the time. Men started to pay more attention to me which really scared me because I didn't want to divorce my husband. That was two years ago. I have since then gained back the seventy pounds and much, much more.

"My life continues to revolve around food. That is all I think about and that is all I do. I don't think about other men anymore. I feel hungry all the time, and I can never get filled up. I don't even seem to think about what I'm eating. Before I know it, I have finished a box of cookies or eaten a quart of ice cream. My grocery bills are astronomical. My husband is more angry at the fact that I am spending money on food than upset about my weight." Fran, like Cathy and Jane, has made food the center of her life.

Fran is the ultimate bad girl. She had an affair with food and an affair with a man and feels guilty about both. Fran has succumbed to the excesses of the flesh and is now paying the price. Like the girls of the 1950s, who gave in and let themselves go all the way, Fran feels guilt, remorse, and self-hate. Like them, she is torn between wanting to satisfy the cravings of her body and wanting to be "good." Try as she may, she cannot control her passions. She pays a heavy price for giving in to her desires: guilt, depression, and self-loathing.

STAGGERING STATISTICS

Eating disorders have been termed the diseases of the 1980s. However, the preoccupation and the obsession with food are not limited to women like Fran, Cathy, and Jane with known eating disorders. In a Gallup survey reported in the *Phoenix Gazette* (Nov. 7, 1985), it was found that almost one of every three women diets at least once a month, and one of six considers herself a perpetual dieter. The survey also found that young U.S. women between the ages of 19 and 39 periodically go on food binges in which they eat extremely high quantities of high-calorie foods in a short space of time. Indeed, binge eating appears to be one of the national sports for college women. Estimates of the prevalence of binge eating in college women have ranged from 54 percent to 86 percent (Ondercin, 1979; Halmi, Falk & Schwartz, 1981; Hawkins & Clement, 1984; Katzman, Wolchik, & Braver, 1984). From these studies, we can see that *two-thirds of college-aged women engage in frequent food binges!* It is clear from these findings that "normal" women without any known eating disorders are frequently binging and dieting.

Some experts feel that eating disorders are reaching epidemic proportions and estimate the national rate to be as high as 12 percent of women. Roughly two million young women suffer from the symptoms of anorexia nervosa or bulimia. Researchers have estimated that about 40 percent of the adult U.S. population is significantly overweight. Although men as well as women are above their ideal weight, in our culture fat is seen as particularly a woman's problem; and thus, eating disorders primarily affect women.

The preoccupation with food and dieting pervades the psychology of women. The alarming numbers of both fasting and binging behaviors reflect the intensity of the double-edged sword. How can a woman satisfy her natural desire to eat and, at the same time, conform to society's demands that she be thin? The fasting reflects the self-denial and deprivation women will undergo to meet the criteria for lovability. The binging is evidence that self-denial does not work.

Chapter 3

Eat and Be Thin

"The way to a man's heart is through his stomach."

"No one will love you if you are fat."

DIET MADNESS

Indeed, Americans seem to be consumed with food. More than at any other time in modern history, women are giving paramount importance to their diet and exercise habits. Researchers have estimated that over 60 percent of U.S. women are dieting at some point in a year, and that number seems to be going up. More than $10 billion a year are spent on diet drugs, diet meals, diet books, exercise tapes, weight-loss classes, and fat farms. Approximately $800 million goes for frozen diet dinners, and another $200 million goes for diet pills. In addition, hundreds of millions of dollars are spent on diet books, health club memberships, and exercise videotapes.

This emphasis on dieting and slimness is reinforced by the media which bombards women daily through television ads, magazines, and billboards with images of the ideal woman and with products on how to achieve this perfection. Diet books occupy more space in bookstores than ever before. In one year of this craze, more than 200 diet books were published. The proliferation of diet books is a recognition of the extent of women's fears of being or becoming fat. The anxiety about becoming fat—and therefore unlovable—is so intense that women will often buy three or four books at one time to quell their fears about gaining weight.

The books are geared to every palate and every lifestyle. Implicit in each is the message that you can satisfy your cravings at the same time that you lose weight. The books assure women that they can fulfill their bodily urges without going wild and succumbing to the ultimate humiliation of being overweight. *The Carbohydrate Craver's Diet* (1984) by Judith J. Wurtman, PhD, announces on the front cover that it is "the first diet that succeeds where others fail because it satisfies your daily needs for sugar and starch." *Rechtschaffen's Diet for Lifetime Weight Control and Better Health* (1980) by Joseph S. Rechtschaffen, M.D. and Robert Carola assures us that "the power to positive eating lets you give up your pounds but not your pasta." All of these books imply that you can have your cake and eat it, too. The authors of these books recognize that central conflict plaguing women: how can they satisfy their need for food and remain slim?

Women are looking for a perfect solution in a perfect diet, one that will allow them to satisfy their cravings without denying themselves. This diet madness is not about food: it is about being lovable and acceptable. It is indicative of women's basic fears that if they let themselves go by eating to their hearts' content, they will be ostracized. So women will diet and deny themselves. Without the love and approval of a partner, they feel worthless.

Diets are not only found in books, but in magazines as well. Women's magazines are the greatest purveyors of the diet mania. Every single woman's magazine has at least one article each month on how to lose weight and become the body beautiful. Some magazines have regular diet columns. Magazines directed at both housewives and career women, and ranging in readership from women with traditional female values, to liberated feminists, feature articles on dieting. Diets appear in magazines for both women with grade school education and those holding PhDs.

Women are bombarded by messages telling them to be slim. Even the woman who does not routinely read books or magazines cannot escape glancing at the latest diet fads as she goes through the checkout counter. If she somehow manages to escape the checkout counters, she can still read about the most recent diet fads in the daily paper. The proliferation of diet literature may compel women to diet, even those who ordinarily would not. The message is that they are not okay the way they are, that they need to trim their waists down and get rid of their flab before they will be found acceptable. The literature preys on women's basic inadequacies and insecurities and heightens their fear that if they do not shape up, they will end up abandoned and alone.

The dieting articles further imply that women who cannot practice self-control in their eating have something drastically wrong with them. For example, an article in the religious section of the *Phoenix Gazette* (Thompson, Nov. 16, 1985) reflected the desperation of those who cannot control their food cravings. The title read: "Faith Can Help Take Fat Off," and described a ministry known as Overeaters Victorious, also referred to as the Jesus Diet. The article stated that "God can help; double-fudge brownies can't." The leader of this movement, disappointed in her lack of success with other weight loss programs, turned to the Bible for help. She explained, "I had been taught from very early childhood that God had the answer for everything.... It just occurred to me as I was reading the Bible one day...that this might be the answer." She implied that overeating is sinful and said that when people are eating out of control, they have some sin in their past which they think is unforgivable. "The Scriptures say the battle of the flesh is always with us," she declared. "Self-control always has to be exercised."

Even the woman who does not leave her house or does not read is not entirely free from being bombarded by the diet mentality. Just by watching television, she can observe slim actresses on soap operas and situation comedies frequently allude to watching their weight. Talk-show host Oprah Winfrey, after losing 67 pounds on a liquid fasting program in 1988, hauled a wagon containing 67 pounds of meat fat onto her stage and proudly showed her awed audience the magnitude of her dieting success. (She has since gained the weight back.) And the commercials between programs constantly bring to the viewer's attention a whole spectrum of diet products which are being consumed by thin, glamorous women. The message is constantly there: "If you eat or drink these diet foods, you too can be slim and gorgeous."

These diet foods take up shelf space in every supermarket and are creating a new dimension to the packaged food industry. Twenty or even ten years ago, diet products were a rarity. Now they are abundant and are consumed in huge quantities. Almost every soft drink has its diet counterpart. The shelves are stocked with Diet Cokes, Diet Pepsis, Diet Root Beers, Diet Seven-Ups, and Diet Sprites in a variety of flavors. Alcoholic beverages also have their low-calorie versions, such as Bud Lite, Miller Lite, and Coors Lite. The whole line of dairy products has gradations of fat and calorie concentrates. One can buy skim milk, one percent, two percent, or whole milk. Cheeses, butters, and yogurts come in skim and low-fat varieties. Meats are also graded according to fat contents, with lean and very lean varieties of cuts. Sweet products are "decalorized," with "low-calorie" ice cream, candy, syrup, and canned fruits as examples. Prepared foods from companies such as Weight Watchers and Lean Cuisine feature entire meals geared specifically for the dieter. Snack foods, such as potato chips and crackers, also come in low-caloried versions, as do sauces, salad dressings, and even mayonnaise.

Women will buy these low-calorie, low-fat products, even at higher prices, because diet foods quell their fears of getting fat and risking their chances of being loved and valued. The manufacturers of diet products recognize women's obsession for slimness together with their very real oral drives, and so they create "safe" foods to cater to all cravings: from "lean" lasagna to "dietetic" chocolate. Loading up a grocery cart with "safe" food provides an illusory—and expensive—solution to the conflict. Many women spend hundreds of dollars on diet food each month so they can eat a variety of food while striving for their goal of having the perfect body.

Diet products do not only come in supermarkets; they are also found in drug stores. The pharmaceutical companies have created a pharmacopaeia of diet aids in liquid, powder, or pill form. The magical properties of these products quell the stirrings of appetite and create the feeling of satiation. Just as saltpeter was used to diminish sexual desire in the army many years ago, so are these products used to curb oral demands. Until recently, amphetamines were prescribed to help women overcome their hunger drives, and scores of dieters took them in spite of their dangerous side effects. Other types of diet pills are readily available over the counter, and in drugstores one is bombarded by a wall of brightly colored packages of different diet pills, each promising to be the magic answer. Shelves of diuretics and laxatives also catch the eye. These products, just like the day-after birth control pill, purge away the sins of the previous day. The most infamous of these is Herbal Life, tablets and powders whose effective purging powers have caused physical damage. Food substitutes, in powder or liquid, formed with specific caloric contents are also sold in drugstores and supermarkets. These canned products set boundaries on appetites and give the feeling of fullness. By following such strict regimens, the dieter cannot let her passions lead her astray.

Research has shown that Americans spend *$200 million* annually on various over-the-counter diet pills. Some drugs, such as amphetamines, inhibit appetite by affecting the brain chemistry. Sales estimates for diet pills were as high as $400 million annually by the early 1990s. Scientists are racking their brains to come up with ideas so that women can have their cake and eat it, too.

FAT FARMS AND OTHER FAT FIGHTERS

There are many organizations that help individuals avoid the temptation of food. One of the best known organizations is Weight Watchers, which makes a business of instructing women in their specific diet plans. Members adhere rigidly to a highly structured plan for limited food intake. At each meeting the members are weighed to see whether they have been good. The atmosphere at these meetings is reminiscent of a 1950s high school milieu where the good—the chaste—reveled in their reward of smug self-righteousness; the bad girls who had indulged had to face the consequence of their behavior, humiliation. Today's women who cannot control their eating, dread the weekly weighing as much as the bad girl of the 1950s dreaded the missed period.

The uncontrollable nature of eating is one of the fundamental principles of Overeaters Anonymous. Women who overeat view themselves as having no control over their consuming passion for food and use the organization as a vehicle for keeping themselves in line. At every meeting, they have to announce their lack of control and their addiction to food. They then give themselves over to a "higher power" who can save them from themselves. Their desire is so great that they need external sources to help them on a daily basis. Women confess their sins at each meeting. Over and over they have to learn not to give in to their lovers: Mr. Goodbar, Baby Ruth, Baskin Robbins, and Haagen Dazs. Their longings are so intense that they call their sponsors daily to help them overcome their need. In addition, they have available to them daily meetings for group support to help them control their cravings.

Group support to battle their love-hate relationship with food is available through other organizations and seminars. TOPS (Take Off Pounds Sensibly), like Overeaters Anonymous and Weight Watchers, is nationwide and provides companionship in the never-ending struggle. Jenny Craig, Nutri System, Diet Center, and Optifast are now everyday household words. In their own ways, these organizations are not very different from all the other diet fads, in that they foster a negative message for a woman. They tell the woman that she is not okay the way she is and teach her relatively painless ways to win the battle of the flesh.

In addition to group support, short-term workshops for compulsive overeaters also provide women with psychological explanations of their overwhelming needs. Geneen Roth, author of *Feeding the Hungry Heart* (1982) and *Breaking Free from Compulsive Eating* (1984), conducts "Breaking Free" workshops for compulsive eaters in Santa Cruz, California. Having been both fat and anorexic herself, she states that one can break free from compulsive eating and can move from being the victim of an uncontrollable desire to a position of choice. Susie Orbach, PhD, a feminist psychotherapist and author of *Fat Is a Feminist Issue* (1978), conducts groups and workshops to help women break their addiction to food. She teaches women to eat whatever they want without depriving themselves, and to make eating a guilt-free and pleasurable experience. Bob Schwartz conducts a DIETS DON'T WORK seminar which is a structured psychological approach to keeping oneself in line and winning the losing battle.

Although the approaches vary, these seminars and workshops all presume that women lack control over their impulses, and their programs aim to help women come to terms with this oral-moral issue. Women need to control themselves; they need to remain "good" girls at all costs. Otherwise, they risk ridicule, ostracism, and abandonment.

The medical and allied professionals also aim to help women curb their appetites. Psychologists and psychiatrists offer individual and group therapy to help women monitor their behavior. Women are taught to record *when* they eat, *what* they eat, and under what conditions they indulge. Through behavior modification, they learn techniques to limit their indulgences. In some programs, they are instructed to chew their food very slowly, as many as 30 times per mouthful, to eat only in specified places, or to put their utensils down after each bite. Through hypnosis, they learn to satisfy themselves with limited quantities of food and to increase their self-control. Bariatric physicians, who exclusively specialize in weight control, offer special products to women to help them in their fight, and monitor them through their fasts and diet programs.

Women's obsession with dieting has become so extreme that hospital administrators have created special inpatient units geared exclusively to the shrinking of American women. The hospital provides a controlled environment where all temptation is removed, and where women can learn new eating habits while they recover from their sinful ways.

For women who prefer a less sterile setting to shed unwanted pounds, health spas, or so-called "fat farms," provide a more luxurious alternative. In tastefully decorated dining rooms, exquisitely prepared morsels of low calorie food are served on beautiful china and crystal. Women exercise from dawn to dusk, and return rejuvenated and five pounds lighter after a week of an intensive all-out effort to fight fat. The battle of the flesh continues.

THE QUEST FOR THE PERFECT BODY

The obsession with food and dieting is also the obsession with having the perfect body, which is thin, muscular, and devoid of fat. At no time in history have women set such stringent and rigid definitions of what their bodies should look like. In a survey of 102,000 women reported in the February 1986 issue of the *Ladies' Home Journal* (Enos and Enos), respondents expressed satisfaction with themselves in most areas of their lives—their intelligence, sexual appeal, ability to handle money—but their greatest dissatisfaction was with their body image. Almost half said that if they could change one thing about themselves, they would want to be thinner.

In another national survey conducted for Weight Watchers, it was concluded that U.S. women were "obsessed" about fitness, nutrition, and dieting. A random sample of 1000 women between the ages of 25 and 54 indicated that four out of five women said they worry more about fitness and weight than they did five years ago. Three out of five exercise at least three times a week, and seven out of ten have dieted at one time or another. Nearly four out of ten see themselves as overweight.

According to a survey on body image reported in *Psychology Today* (Cash, Winstead and Janda 1986), Americans, although healthier and fitter than ever, said they were less satisfied with how they looked. Women were generally more critical of their bodies than men were of theirs. Fifty-five percent of the women were dissatisfied with their weight; 63 percent were afraid of getting fat. The results of the survey support the notion that women hold rather extreme standards for an acceptable body. In holding to this relentlessly thin standard to determine their attractiveness, their chances for having a good body image are very low.

Although standards of what constitutes an attractive body have varied over the years, at no other time has anorexic-like slimness been held up as the model of physical beauty. The ideal body type for women today is boyishly thin, devoid of curves and sexless. Recently, in the local newspapers, one reader wanted to know whether Princess Stephanie of Monaco was a boy or a girl. The princess is a prototype of the woman of today: thin, sinewy, angular, small-breasted, and a size 3.

Is there life after size 3? Not judging by all of the bodies seen on television, billboards, and magazine covers. The royal road to the perfect body is paved with exercise, with aerobics being the bedrock, and "step-classes" a close second. Vigorous aerobics can work off more calories per minute than any other form of exercise, offering an efficient way to achieve the perfect body.

Aerobics classes are ubiquitous, appearing in churches, schools, hospitals and corporate settings, as well as in regular studios and health spas. The trendy Yuppie carries her aerobics bag to the office and works out at least twice a week. Exercise records and videos abound, so that the woman can exercise at her own leisure if she does not want to join a class. Women are constantly reminded to "get in shape" by the large number of books, records, and videotapes which are prominently displayed in the front of the store. Famous movie stars lead women in their search for thinness through their exercise routines. The most well-known of these is Jane Fonda, who used to have an eating disorder and now has workout studios, as well as several books and tapes on how to attain the perfect body. No woman is excused or immune from shaping up, with workouts designed for younger, older, and even pregnant women. Debbie Reynolds holds out hope for the older and out-of-shape women by telling them to "Do it Debbie's Way."

Magazine articles constantly emphasize the importance of having a perfect body. Their titles remind women of their imperfections and create guilt about not meeting standards of thinness. Two articles in the June 1985 issue of *Mademoiselle,* "How to Make Your Body Bare-able," and "Legs Are Back! Can You Bare Them?" imply that the body is not acceptable the way it is and cannot be exposed to others. It needs constant shaping up. It is hard to escape the guilt and shame that comes from having a body that will never attain the standards of perfection. Almost every woman's magazine has at least one article that focuses on the body, an article such as "Get a New You Now" (*Glamour,* October 1988), "Trim Thighs, Tummy, Hips in Just 3 Weeks!" (*Family Circle,* June 5, 1990), "Spas: The New Habit Formers" (*Vogue,* December 1988), "Big Hips? Bulging Thighs? 6 Quickie Exercises" (*Redbook,* October 1990) and, "How to Look 10 lbs. Thinner on the Beach" (*Ladies' Home Journal,* June 1988).

The preoccupation with having a perfect body is so pronounced that there are magazines devoted solely to that topic. *New Body* tells its readers how to exercise and eat so that they can look like glamorous models and be fit. *Shape* focuses on total fitness for the active woman. The message is loud and clear: being slim is one of the most important things in life. No matter how busy, how hectic, or how harassed you are, you need to take the time to exercise, diet, and develop that perfect body. Articles tell you how to work out before, after, and during work—even at your desk, as explained in *Shape*'s November 1985 issue in "Don't Just Sit There - Fit Tips for Desk Workers (Taylor, Delong and Freisinger). It is not enough to simply put your mind to work—you must simultaneously contract your abdominal muscles, tense up your thighs, and mold and fashion the rest of your body. You can exercise while driving, flying, or waiting in line—no opportunity should be missed to achieve the perfect body.

It has been said that there are no fat women, only lazy ones. Indeed, thinness carries with it a myriad of connotations. Not just the opposite of being lazy, being thin symbolizes self-control and restraint. The trim body makes a statement: here is a woman who is in charge of her life, a woman who knows how to say no to her most primitive impulses. Being slim is a metaphor for self-restraint, deprivation, and will power. It reflects the ability to resist temptation and to not succumb to the excesses of the flesh. To be thin is to be pure, moral, and perfect—in short, to be the ultimate good girl. And to be good is to be loved and respected.

Actress Diahann Carroll is a perfect example of the "good girl" image. Diahann's svelte, toned, leotarded body appeared on the cover of the November 1985 issue of *Shape*, in which a feature article on her appeared (Cross). "She can count on a 12- to 14-hour day at least two days a week," said the article, sometimes even five days, but she fits in exercise classes whenever she has a moment. She found many years ago that she needed someone to make a study of her body and its needs so that her squeezed-in workouts would be efficient. So she has the luxury of a personal trainer, Karen Voight of the Voight Fitness Center in West Hollywood, who has been working with her for many years. Karen comes to her house, sometimes as late as 10:00 p.m., for an hour and half workout. As much as Diahann would like to take a shower and hit the sack, she knows that her hard-worked body needs attention...Diahann admits to not being an exercise lover." How can you exercise vigorously ... for an hour and a half...at 10:00 p.m....after a 12- or 14-hour workday...when you do not even like exercise?!

Diahann's diet regimen appears to be just as stringent. Although she does not "diet" per se, she does have certain dietary rules: "She never eats anything fried or anything with white flour or sugar in it; she avoids salt.... Alcohol intake is moderated; she does not permit herself hard liquor and drinks, only wine—and adores champagne. When she knows she will have champagne, she is very careful before, and will drink nothing and eat very little." Any evidence of indulging in the delights of food is quickly eradicated. She constantly wards off the effects of oral gratification by "walking" around the house on her fanny and works her arms as she drives.

EXTREME MEASURES

For women who lack Diahann's superhuman self-control, modern medicine offers surgical alternatives. Women who detest sit-ups can now have their tummies tucked in for an average cost of $2000 to $3500. In this procedure, the fat from the stomach is taken out, and the remains of past indulgences are aborted. When the sins of over-eating manifest themselves in the thighs and rear ends, they can be suctioned out in a rather painful procedure called a lipectomy, or liposuction. In this surgery, a thin tube is inserted into an over-fat area of the body and, with the aid of a vacuum-like device, the fat is suctioned out. A bulging thigh, stomach or hip can be flattened in a fairly simple procedure, which may explain why liposuction has become one of the most frequent types of cosmetic surgery performed in the United States today. Despite the pain, the risks of complications, and the high cost which is not covered by insurance, more and more *average weight women* are flocking to plastic surgeons to suction out their fat. The costs of being thin and lovable can be very high.

Women who have thrown caution to the winds, lost control completely, and let their passions consume them have to resort to more drastic alternatives such as Maxilia-mandibular fixation, commonly known as jaw wiring. This current medical device, modelled after the chastity belt, is a cast metal or cap splint cemented to the teeth, with elastic bands attached to the upper and lower splints, to prevent any jaw movement. Thus, the dangerous orifice is effectively closed off. The woman who has her jaws wired announces to the world her powerlessness over her drives.

Her more sensitive sisters, who do not want the public humiliation inherent in jaw wiring, can choose stomach stapling or intestinal bypass surgery. Stomach stapling decreases the capacity of the stomach and limits food intake, while intestinal bypass surgery shortens the absorption surface of the small intestines, thus reducing the amount of calories consumed. Women run the risk of mortality under the surgeon's knife today just as their impassioned and desperate sisters risked their lives seeking illegal abortions many years ago. The surgeon's knife eradicated the badness, the consequences of their immoral behavior.

The extremes to which women will go to achieve perfection under the surgeon's knife is satirized by Fay Weldon in her book *The Life and Loves of a She-Devil* (1981). The protagonist is the antithesis of the modern desirable young woman: she is unusually tall, heavy-boned, ugly, clumsy, and fat. Despite being a compassionate and attentive wife and mother, she loses her husband to the idealized modern woman, a successful writer who is "small and pretty and delicately formed." The heroine goes to considerable lengths to seek revenge and get her husband back, including spending thousands of dollars and many years of torturous pain to become the epitome of feminine perfection. She undergoes multiple surgeries to shorten her body, redo her facial structure, and remodel her contours. The extremes of plastic surgery are described in the book: "That June they started on her torso. They fined down and abbreviated the shoulder blades. They made the breasts smaller. They removed flesh from the upper arms and drew the loose skin up into the armpits. They liquidized and drew off fat from the dowager's hump that had developed at the base of her neck. They moved downward. They tautened and lifted her belly and tightened her buttocks" (p. 253). The heroine eventually becomes addicted to heroin to dull the pain, but the physical, emotional, and financial costs of the surgeries are a small price to pay for the rewards of bodily perfection and the return of the husband's devotion!

Unfortunately, in real life, achieving bodily perfection does not guarantee love and happiness. In our studies of patients who had undergone intestinal bypass surgery, we found that many of them developed very serious psychological problems after losing their fat, including anorexia, depression, and even psychosis.

Dora expected miracles when she underwent intestinal bypass surgery. Like the heroine in *The Life and Loves of a She-Devil*, Dora was deserted by her husband for another woman. She felt that her 313 lb. frame had driven him away, and she decided to get rid of all of her excess fat. But her story did not have a happy ending. Athough the surgery was successful and she lost a considerable amount of weight she became severely depressed. She realized that her expectations of what life would be as a thin person were not being met and that weight loss did not compensate for the lack of a husband or feelings of insecurity. As she said, "I thought if the fat would go away, the world would be beautiful. I found that the fat has gone away, but the world is not perfect."

Beth also sought bodily perfection through surgery. Beth was not always heavy, but when she left home to go to college, she developed an enormous appetite and ate her troubles away. Whenever she had an exam or a paper, she headed for the refrigerator. It seemed to her that every pound she gained went directly to her breasts. She began to hate her breasts because men were staring at them. She kept away from men because she thought they only wanted one thing. Soon she started to focus all of her anger on her breasts and blamed them for everything that was going wrong in her life. Finally, she could not tolerate them any longer and had a surgeon reduce their size. Beth still hates her breasts; only now she focuses on the ugly, red surgical scars instead of their size. She still keeps away from men—only now the reason is her belief that no man can love her with such ugly scars.

Beth, Dora, and others are extreme examples of the lengths to which women go to achieve bodily perfection. Dieting, strenuous exercise, and surgery are all attempts to be thin and lovable. The underlying theme is that to be thin is to be valued, to be thin is to be happy, to be thin is to be accepted, to be thin is to be loved.

Isn't it a shame that women will go to such lengths to be loved? Isn't it sad that so many of us believe that our only value rests on the shape and size of our physical proportions? The extremes to which we will go in our quest for bodily perfection is a sad commentary on our society which places so much emphasis on thinness. It is disappointing that in spite of the achievements made by the women's movement, women still place so little value on their worth.

THE DOUBLE MESSAGE

A double message is being broadcast to women today. The conflicting message is to partake in gourmet delights and yet remain thin and desirable. DIET programs, DIET pills, DIET books, DIET food substitutes, DIET powders...no matter where you turn. The message is loud and clear: thin is in, and dieting is the road to happiness. At the same time, there are a plethora of cookbooks and a preoccupation with good food. Happiness is buying a chocolate lover's cookbook and indulging in a chocolate covered strawberry. The double message—to eat, on the one hand, and to remain slim on the other—creates confusion and ambivalence. This paradox is expressed very well in the poem *My Mother's Prayer,* by Linda Myer, in Geneen Roth's book *Feeding the Hungry Heart* (pp. 164-165):

> Eat and be thin.
> Eat and be thin.
> Eat, my child,
> eat and be thin.

The third stanza intensifies the conflict:

> But don't eat too much,
> for if you do,
> you will be fat,
> you will be ugly.
> You will be fat,
> you will be lonely.
> No one will love you
> if you are fat.
> No one will *have* you
> if you are fat.
> Eat, my child,
> eat and be thin.

The double message sings out in every issue of women's magazines. The June 1988 issue of *Vogue* featured an ad for a new dessert cookbook from *Gourmet,* followed by an article for cutting fat from diets. Women are first told to be good girls: then they are seduced with a tantalizing array of fattening desserts. The September 1990 cover of *Ladies' Home Journal* had two features, one following the other. The first read, ''So Long, Saddlebags! Thin Thighs Three

Ways.'' Across the top it read, ''What's Cooking Coast to Coast.''
For every diet feature, there are several recipes, pictures, and articles that tempt, seduce and stimulate the salivary glands. The food
features entice women to gastronomic ecstasy; the diet features warn:
Don't indulge—be pure. As one woman put it, ''I don't know which
is worse—to be fat or to be hungry.''

The dilemma is highlighted by a trip to any major bookstore where
diet books and cookbooks compete for the buyer's attention. Books
telling women to control their appetites are displayed next to
cookbooks whose covers invite women to indulge. Sensuous, mouth-
watering pictures of strawberry shortcakes, chocolate mousse, and
French pastries are displayed in technicolor. The images tease and
titillate, promising ecstasy. A series of books tempt the palate from
foreplay to finish, from tasty appetizers to the main course, followed
by luscious desserts. Within arms' reach are books demanding
abstinence. Diet books of all shapes and sizes urge women to remain
pure and virginal.

The conflict between indulgence and abstinence is reactivated with
every trip to the supermarket. Candies, cookies, gourmet and junk
foods abound, inviting women to pick them up and put them in their
carts. Some of these products are so irresistibly displayed that a
woman has to arm herself against them so that she does not fall under
their spell. She is cautioned to protect herself by eating before
she enters this den of iniquity. We all know never to go grocery
shopping on an empty stomach. A woman needs every ounce of self-
control to walk past the ''bad'' food—aisles and aisles of it—to the
celery and carrots. If she manages to escape the perils of the ''bad''
food, she must exert even greater self-control at the check-out counter
where racks of candy and chocolate are within easy reach. These
are displayed side by side with calorie counters, and other booklets
telling you how to flatten your stomach or trim your thighs. In
addition, different magazines vie for her attention: *Bon Appetit* and
Shape stand side by side . . . ''Eat and be thin, my child, eat and
be thin.''

Nowhere is this conflict more clearly highlighted than on television. Alternating images of beautiful, thin people and mouth-watering
food flash on the screen, creating both the desire to look slim and
the desire to eat. Candy bar ads feature rich, dark, thick chocolate

pouring out and wrapping itself around peanuts and caramel, followed by images of people's faces as they put these candy bars in their mouths. The ecstatic expressions tell all. These images excite the oral appetite, much as pornography excites the sexual appetite. Together with the abundance of food images are beautiful people immaculately groomed and *thin*. Their lives are filled with love, intrigue, romance, and passion. The message is repeated on every show: if you are thin, you will be loved and pursued by men. The arousal of the desire for the perfect body, on the one hand, and the desire to indulge in oral fantasies, on the other, creates a never-ending conflict.

The problem becomes painfully acute for the woman who is involved in a new romantic relationship. To attract her new lover, she believes she must offer him a perfect, slim body. She wonders if he will find her sexually desirable, and she goes to great lengths to camouflage any of her perceived imperfections. However, the rituals of a beginning courtship involve long romantic dinners, usually with before and after dinner drinks, appetizers, and desserts. She also knows that "the way to a man's heart is through his stomach", and attempts to win him through her tempting cuisine. That means no more Lean Cuisines...now it is gourmet delights from the Italian and French cookbooks, including butters, sauces, breads, and creamy rich desserts. And if he stays over, the morning cup of coffee becomes bacon and eggs, or at least croissants or bagels and cream cheese. At the time when she is most interested in a man and most motivated to have a perfect body, she is also forced to embark on an eating orgy to spend time with him and to keep him happy. This seemingly unresolvable dilemma makes it easy to understand why so many women get into destructive dietary patterns.

Are women aware that they are getting two conflicting signals? Do we realize that we are getting paradoxical messages...to eat and to remain slim...to cook gourmet meals and to stay fashionably thin...to have sophisticated tastebuds but to refrain from using them? Apparently not or we would have rebelled by now. As usual, we are trying to please everybody and to meet two opposing demands at the same time. Of course we find ourselves in a quandary, one that seems to have no solution.

AN AGE-OLD DILEMMA

The conflict—to eat or not to eat—is not really about eating. It is about being "good" and being lovable. It is the dilemma of how we can meet our most basic needs and still be loved. It is an age-old conflict between dependence and self-expression. Do I dare please myself and risk losing at love? Can I be responsive to my needs and still have a relationship? If you have to be thin to be in a relationship, then dieting becomes a way of life. It is not the fat on the thighs that is at issue, but a woman's femaleness. Being female means pleasing others and depriving yourself. It means conforming to the standards of lovability, whether these be a size 3 figure or an intact hymen.

Women's needs to be loved and accepted are so strong that they have been willing to resort to extreme measures such as denying their biological drives. The loneliness and isolation that plagues them today is very real. Women fear that they cannot find a man unless they are slim and beautiful. The terror of ending up alone and unloved makes them engage in destructive, self-defeating behavior.

To eat or not to eat has replaced the sexual conflict that plagued women thirty years ago. How can I give in to my desires and still find a man to love me? How can I satisfy my needs without becoming a "bad" girl? How can I take care of me and still find happiness?

How did we get to this state, where food has replaced sex as the foremost realm of conflicting desires for women? In the next chapter, we describe the conflict as it applied to women sexually 30 years ago: to do "it" or not to do "it," and what that meant to the women caught in that dilemma.

Chapter 4

To Do It or Not To Do It

Incessantly, we grappled with the conflicting signals of sex as forbidden, dirty, dangerous, to be denied and lied about but also romantic, exciting and glamourous.

—Benita Eisler, *Private Lives*

How did we get to a state where we are obsessed with food instead of sex? Why had food replaced sex as the foremost conflict in our minds? What has happened in our minds to create this shift? Has the obsession with food merely replaced the obsessions with sex or are they both part of the same phenomenon? Could they possibly be symptoms of the same underlying conflict? We think so. To understand this strange state of affairs, we need to take a look at the changing roles of women in modern history.

SEX IS ONLY FOR MOTHERS

Women in the pre-industrial world had few options. Their role was clear-cut: that of wife and mother. If a woman worked, it was primarily domestic work and then only in unusual circumstances, such as the death of her husband. The industrial revolution brought women to the cities where they started working outside the home and attending school. However, they were expected to marry after they finished school; housewifery was their career. A high school education for girls was thought to improve their mothering abilities.

When colleges opened their doors to women, a small minority chose careers instead of marriage, usually careers that would not take away from their traditional roles, such as teaching and nursing. Colleges perpetuated the traditional female roles of nurturance and unselfishness. Educators advocated the "professionalism of motherhood" so that women were taught to be the best mothers they could.

The few "new" women who resisted the traditional roles were viewed as selfish. Even psychologists supported the view that the only correct role for women was marriage and maternity. As Stanley Hall, a noted psychologist wrote: "It is, to say the very least, not yet proven that the higher education of woman is not injurious to her health" (1904). He also feared that if women waited until they were older to have children, their breasts would dry up from lack of use and their children would be deprived.

A woman's sexuality was closely tied to her main role: motherhood. Birth control was unavailable, and the main purpose of sex was procreation. Women were warned against the expression of their sexuality outside of marriage, and masturbation was forbidden. In some instances women were given clitoridectomies to put a stop to this heinous crime of self-abuse. Sex was clearly not for enjoyment, and women were kept ignorant about their bodies. There was little sexual education for either males or females, and it was not uncommon for young women to experience pain with intercourse because of their fear of the unknown. Most women disliked sex and saw it as their marital duty. Mothers told their daughters to lie down, close their eyes, and think of "something pleasant." Sex was often a nightmare of physical pain for women since the knowledge of foreplay, clitoral arousal, and lubrication was absent. A young girl of that time, speaking of her wedding night, said, "I'm afraid. I'm afraid. I'd like to have myself chloroformed" (Gay, 1984, p. 292).

The twentieth century marked the beginning of a trend for women to attend high school and college in large numbers. This century was also marked by increasing feminist activity which, ultimately, gave women the right to vote in 1920. As women became more educated, many of them began thinking about having careers and becoming more independent. Their desire to be independent was reflected in their sexuality. Although sex still continued to be marriage-oriented and defined by strict standards, middle class women defied their Victorian ancestors and started experimenting with premarital sexual activity. College women in the 1920s engaged in heavy petting but for the most part avoided intercourse. Birth control was still unavailable, and they feared becoming pregnant. In addition, virginity was highly valued, and a woman's reputation was at stake if she had premarital intercourse. Petting was a compromise between keeping old standards while exploring their sexuality. This exploration was characteristic of the risk-taking mood of the 1920s.

The affluent mood of the 1920s was brought to a sobering halt with the crash of the stock market in 1929. Women dropped out of school, were forced out of the limited job market, and retreated into domesticity. This trend continued through the 1940s and into the 1950s. Although women returned to work during World War II, this was a patriotic endeavor rather than a move toward liberation from traditional roles. When their men returned from war, women marched back into the home and their house dresses. For those women who did work, the job market became rigidly segregated, with primarily "women's jobs" available to them: teaching, secretarial, nursing, or social work. Technical and professional jobs were taken over by men, and women's earning power declined. Women, if they worked, shaped their work around their family life.

The traditional value of home and motherhood reemerged with the return of lovers and husbands from the war, and women got busy once again making babies. This was the beginning of the Baby Boom, and everything became focused on making the home the center of a woman's life. The American dream was for her to have a husband, home, and children. All over the country, tract housing became available, and kitchen and laundry appliances were developed.

The ideal woman of the post-war era could be found in her immaculate kitchen surrounded by her automatic washer and dryer, mixers and cookbooks, as she baked cookies from the latest Betty Crocker recipe. The "happy homemaker" divided her time between cooking, sewing, cleaning, and child care. Her social life revolved around her husband and home and daily coffee klatches with her neighbors discussing their children and the latest recipes.

To be a wife and mother was the only goal to which a young girl aspired, and all of her dreams and hopes revolved around finding a husband who would take care of her and with whom she would live happily ever after. Colette Dowling, (1981), calls this phenomenon the "Cinderella complex." A young girl's activity was geared toward that goal, which was to be achieved as early as possible. She was beseiged by fears of becoming an old maid. Being popular with the opposite sex was more important than academic success, and women who were pinned or engaged in high school were the envy of their girlfriends.

Husband-hunting continued on the college campus, where women pursued the "Mrs. Degree." If a woman reached 25 with no marriage prospects, she became distraught about her fate. Women who did not go to college took stop-gap secretarial jobs until they landed their man. It was not long before love and marriage were followed by a baby carriage because children were the ultimate fulfillment of a young girl's wishes and dreams. To be a wife and mother was the woman's socially appropriate role, and her sexuality was only sanctioned within the confines of that role.

DON'T TOUCH "DOWN THERE"

For women before the sexual revolution, sexuality was laden with fear, guilt, and fascination. Sex was a subject that was taboo and not discussed anywhere. There were no books or magazine articles that were readily available for a young girl to read. The few marriage manuals that she could get her hands on were secretly consumed under the bedcovers. Much of the information was worthless, just like the junk food of the contemporary adolescent. She had nobody to talk to about the secret workings of her body or the delicious sensations she may have experienced if she dared let herself experiment.

Alix Shulman describes how it was for the young girl in *Memoirs of an Ex-Prom Queen* (1969):

> Between my legs I had found an invisible button of flesh, sweet and nameless, which I knew how to caress to a nameless joy. I was pretty sure no one else had one, for there was no joy button in the hygiene book and there was not even a dirty name for it. Though I listened carefully, I never heard anyone, boy or girl, so much as allude to it, nor was it pictured on the diagram in the Kotex box. Once, my anxiety overcoming my embarrassment, I had tried to ask my friend Jackie about it. But lacking a name or description for it, I couldn't even present the subject. When Jackie simply looked at me blankly, little beads of shame dampened my forehead, and I shut up. After that, I never dared question anyone (p. 46).

There was a great deal of mystery surrounding female anatomy. Female genitals were referred to as "down there," with the implication that they were somehow shameful and forbidden to explore. When a mother admonished her daughter to be sure to wash "down there," she also gave her the message that her genitals had to be cleansed and purged of their natural odor and dirt. Implicit in the admonition was that it was *dirty* and *bad* "down there," that we wash it, but that we do not talk about it. Women were both fearful and fascinated about exploring their bodies. The brave few poked around tentatively; the rest merely wondered.

Anything connected with "down there" was taboo and it is no surprise that mothers did not prepare their daughters for menstruation. The first period was usually traumatic, as Shulman aptly describes: "One day I got out of the bath bleeding *down there,* and from the nervous way my mother said it was 'natural' after I screamed for her from the bathroom, I knew for sure I was a freak" (p. 42).

Various euphemisms such as "the time of month," "the curse," "falling off the roof" or "a visit from my friend" referred to menstruation. Words specifically describing female sexuality were never said out loud, but were clouded, reinforcing the ignorance and mystery surrounding the whole area. Brown paper wrappers covered Kotex boxes which were carefully hidden in the back rooms of drug stores. Whispers and blushes characterized any reference to the workings of the female genitalia.

SEXUAL IGNORANCE

The mystery and lack of knowledge created a constant preoccupation with sex and sexuality. Not having any factual knowledge, women dreaded sex and were at the same time fascinated by the possibility of having intercourse. Women both worried and fantasized about their wedding nights. Having been raised with romantic novels and songs, they were ignorant of the genital and sexual side of marriage. Many women had never seen an erect penis and were scared by its size. Being ignorant of female anatomy, they worried whether it was big enough "down there" to accommodate it. They also feared the pain that was only whispered about. In addition, they had no knowledge of how to get aroused and relied solely on their also ignorant husbands to get them ready. Frequently, this combination of mutual ignorance led to pain and disappointment for the woman.

This state of affairs persisted well into marriage. Sexual satisfaction was thought to develop over time. Even doctors took this view, as illustrated in an article in the July 1955 issue of *Ladies' Home Journal* (Adams). The doctor in this case quotes a young wife: "The first two years of our marriage were happy, and I never doubted Jim's love until about a year ago. Then he started suggesting certain things when we made love that seem wrong or unnatural. So far I've given in, but I feel terribly guilty and ashamed. He's a good husband in most ways, but I can't believe he'd treat me like this if he respected me." The doctor advised that: "During the first year or so of marriage, many young couples do not achieve a satisfactory sexual adjustment." He adds that "sexual responsiveness usually develops later and more slowly in women than in men" and explains that, "many young wives, though they talk glibly of textbook learning, have little real knowledge and understanding of sex."

Even women who had some knowledge of genital sex often found the realities of sexual relations a shock and responded with disgust and aversion. In the January 1954 issue of *Cosmopolitan*, an article titled "Romance Can Ruin Your Marriage" (Lagemann) speaks to this issue. The author recognized that even educated women had romantic and unrealistic notions about sex. He talked about women who become repelled and disgusted by the realities of sexual intercourse, even though they had read the Kinsey Report and had talked to their fiances about sex prior to marriage. They experience a terrific let-down and the feeling of "Is this all there is?"

For the majority of women, sexual intercourse did not result in sexual satisfaction. They were often disappointed that "the earth didn't move," and the only thing that happened was that they got their hair messed up. What they thought to be an earth-shattering expression of love frequently turned out to be a messy, inconvenient, and sometimes painful experience. The sex act did not naturally bring about joy and ecstasy as women had read about in novels and romantic stories. Implicit in the romance literature was the notion that good sex came naturally and flowed from love. If you were truly in love, sex would be perfect. The man was supposed to know exactly what to do to bring his princess to fulfillment. Unfortunately, neither the prince nor the princess had the skills and knowledge to bring about sexual bliss.

Myths and misconceptions abounded. What was written about female sexuality was in romantic rather than in factual or anatomical language: "She went soft and spineless in his arms, the ice of her pride melting. 'Don't go, Olaf!'" (Kennelly in *Ladies' Home Journal*, July 1955, p. 52). No information is given on arousal, lubrication, or orgasm. It is assumed that if you meet the right man and you are in love, you will melt in his arms and ecstasy will follow. Very few women knew that they had a clitoris, let alone understood its role in sexual satisfaction, and even those educated women who had read about or discovered their "joy button" believed that orgasm was produced only by the penis entering the vagina. The followers of Freud, the psychoanalysts, and the medical profession reinforced this view by stating that the only correct way to orgasm was through sexual intercourse. Sigmund Freud distinguished between clitoral and vaginal orgasms, stating that only immature, neurotic women achieved orgasms through clitoral stimulation. The healthy, fulfilled woman had orgasms the "right" way: through intercourse. Women who had not gone to college or were not familiar with Freudian thinking relied on books and magazines for information about their sexuality, but practical information was virtually nonexistent. Even so-called "liberal" books like Helen Gurley Brown's *Sex and the Single Girl* (1962), which condoned premarital sex, did not provide explicit sexual information.

FAKING ORGASMS

Men, who were believed to be the authorities on sex, were just as misinformed as women. They believed that as soon as the woman got wet, she was ready for intercourse. All that was required were a few thrusts of the penis, and they would achieve their goal: Simultaneous Orgasm. True romantic love required that the man and woman come at exactly the same moment in a frenzy of pulsating passion.

These unrealistic expectations resulted in bitter disappointment or faked orgasms. Women relied on what they had read about in romance novels to play out the role of a sexually aroused woman. Just as heroines moaned and groaned and writhed from sheer ecstasy, so too did American women perform their sexual dance. Women faked because they did not know what an orgasm was, but they knew that they had to feel *something* and do *something*. The worst thing you could do was lie there like a limp rag, so women learned to become sexual actresses, continuing to reinforce the myth that a few thrusts of the penis were enough to drive any woman crazy with ecstasy. Men were chagrined many years later to read in the *Hite Report* (1976) that about 54 percent of the women surveyed said they faked orgasms and that their wifely expressions of bliss were merely well-staged performances. As one woman stated on the survey, "I did it until we were married because I thought getting married would do the trick. Ha!" Another said; "Yes, it's easier and faster than struggling."

Not all women faked orgasm, of course. Many women "just had a headache" a great deal of the time. Sex surveys from that period indicated that only half the married women in the United States experienced orgasms with any consistency. This means that one out of two married women experienced frustration and disappointment in most of her sexual encounters. The Kinsey Report (1953) on female sexuality claimed that one of the reasons why women did not achieve orgasm is the "female's inexperience in orgasms prior to her marriage" (p. 172). The women who had found their clitoris through masturbation prior to marriage were those few who did have orgasms after marriage.

Although masturbation was considered sinful by some religions and at best "bad" or "wrong," some young women reached up under their night clothes and found their "joy buttons." This activity was always done in an atmosphere of guilt, shame, and fear of terrible consequences, as Alix Shulman describes it:

> At night in bed I would swear to caress my joy button only once, and then, breaking my promise, give myself up to it. I expected something terrible to happen, but I couldn't help it. Trying to control my controlling obsession, I led myself into

strange nocturnal rituals and odd compulsions. The more I would prolong my caress before my joy button 'went on', the more often I allowed myself to stroke it. I would count the strokes and try to break my record. I was torn between prolonging the joy and getting it over with before I heard my parents coming upstairs. (p. 46)

Alix Shulman's description of the secrecy surrounding masturbation is characteristic of the forbidden nature of sexual expression at that time. Sex was both forbidden and unattainable, a subject of fantasy and mystery, with the promise of delicious ecstasy at some illusive future time. The combination of ignorance surrounding sex and its clandestine nature led women to constantly think, fantasize, and dream about it.

THE SWEET MYSTERY OF LOVE

Sex in the 1950s could not be separated from the romantic illusions that cloaked it. Just as today's woman cannot escape being bombarded by visions of the perfect body, her mother was constantly exposed to themes of love and romance. It was believed, though not explicitly stated, that if you were in love with the *right* man, good sex would naturally follow. The ultimate romantic fantasy was that two lovers would merge, their passion culminating in a breathtaking moment of ecstasy: the simultaneous orgasm. No mention was ever made of such mundane concerns as when he should "put it in," when she should insert the diaphragm, whether to wash the drippy semen off or not, and what to do if she did not come.

The implicit promise that with the right man, happiness would follow, is the same message promised today by every diet fad: one day you will be thin, and happiness will follow. Your whole life will magically change, and you will live happily ever after. The promise was held out, with the hope of the magical transformation.

These hopes and dreams were kept alive by the books, songs, and movies of that era. Baritones crooned their way into the hearts of millions of love-struck young women, their songs filled with themes of true love, innocent and eternal. The magic of romance flowed through "Some Day My Prince Will Come" or "Some Enchanted Evening." There was one special unique person just for you, who had the power to change your life, to transform it to ecstasy if you were fortunate enough to have him. Over and over, women listened: "It had to be you, wonderful you." Love was the be-all and end-all of a woman's existence.

In films as well, sex was idealized and romanticized and never explicity described or discussed. There were no scenes of a man and a woman sleeping together in the same bed, even when they were married. Scenes of nudity were nonexistent, and lovemaking was limited to romantic kisses. The hero's hand never travelled below the neck, and four-letter words never passed his lips. Even movies with sultry heroines engaged in sexual liaisons did not openly depict or discuss explicit sexual behavior. Although Ava Gardner, Lana Turner, and other sexy actresses appeared sensuous and alluring on film, they never exposed their breasts and limited their lovemaking to activities above the neck. Actors generated a great deal of heat and passion without taking their clothes off and engaging in any explicit sexual activity. The intense lovemaking was only hinted at by heavy breathing, providing fuel for the fantasy of the viewers and lingering on long after the film was over.

KEEPING THE HYMEN INTACT AT ALL COSTS

Women fantasized about the delights of intercourse which they would experience when they married Mr. Right, for they knew that they could only taste the fruits of ecstasy after marriage—provided they had not spoiled themselves. They knew they had to remain "pure" or they would lose their reputation and no man would marry them. Thus, they learned not to squander their sexual goods, because the consequences of being a "bad" girl were horrendous. If a woman lost her "good girl" status, she would be talked about, ridiculed, and ostracized. She would risk never getting married which at that time was more horrible than one could think about. As Carol Cassell writes in *Swept Away* (1984):

Once the line was crossed and the hymen punctured, marriage had better be in the future, the immediate future. The girl who broke this convention was labelled, objectified; her value as a person was attacked. Cheap. Trash. Terms applied to worthless commodities. Whore. Slut.... The harsh judgment behind those overwrought epithets is a clue to the sizable investment our culture has made in keeping women Good Girls. (p. 93)

Women had to exercise restraint over their sexual appetites lest they go out of control. They would carefully portion out their sexual pleasures, never entirely permitting themselves to binge. Sexual favors were carefully measured, doled out bit by bit. Women decided before each date just how many sexual delights they could allow themselves, just as today they mentally prepare themselves before going out to dinner. They spent hours thinking, planning, and fantasizing over how much of the forbidden fruit they could consume. Just as women today count out the calories of what they have taken in, women then kept track of how far they had gone with each date and how much more they could afford to splurge. A binge could result in disaster: not only did a woman risk losing her reputation, she could get pregnant as well.

In her book, Shulman quotes *Girls Alive*:

If you kiss Mike tonight, the next time you go out with him, it will be natural to kiss him again. Each date with him you may go a little further in what will become a dangerous game...

Meanwhile, you will go out with other boys and it's easy enough to slip into the same habits with them. In no time you have earned yourself the reputation of being a girl any man can kiss. (pp. 73-74)

For a woman to keep her hymen intact was no easy feat—no easier than keeping a size 5 figure. It required constant vigilance against the body's hungers. Both internal and external forces pressured the woman not to give in. Necking and petting whetted the appetite, but then she had to stop, and not cross the line into gluttony. Her boyfriend's constant pressure to "go all the way," and his promise of how wonderful it would be only intensified the hunger. He would offer her a sample of the pleasures to come. "I'll only put it in a little bit," he would promise. The constant pressure to have sex on the one hand, while remaining a virgin on the other created an ongoing battle within the woman, intensifying the preoccupation and hunger. Women were caught up in a perpetual conflict. Those who succumbed would promise themselves that they would never do it again. Periods of indulgence were followed by guilt and remorse which only heightened the preoccupation and obsession.

PETTING: THE AGONY AND THE ECSTASY

For the majority of women who did not succumb, petting provided some means of sexual satisfaction without losing one's virginity. Petting was the primary sexual activity for unmarried women, with different gradations and progressions depending on the length and seriousness of the relationship. Sexual activity would start out with kissing which would easily evolve into French kissing. French kissing invariable led to petting above the waist and ultimately to petting below the waist.

It took much force of will to stop just before the ultimate step. As one woman described it:

"We went as far as we could without going all the way. He would keep begging for more each time, and each time it became harder and harder to say no. Before we would go out, I would be obsessed with what we would do at the end of the evening, how far I would go and how I could keep myself in control. I would mentally prepare myself by saying over and over in my mind that I would only go up to a certain point. I would rehearse the words I would say to him as a way of gaining control over both our passions. I would spend much of my waking time alternately fantasizing about sex and then devising ways to keep it within bounds."

Petting was like being on a constant diet where restraint and control always had to be exercised. Some women were on stricter diets than others, not permitting themselves the pleasures of petting below the waist. Different gradations of petting were permitted on different occasions or with different guys, just as on special occasions women allowed themselves to overeat.

SEX IS ALWAYS ON MY MIND

Women of the 1950s were love-struck. Thousands of starry-eyed women walked out of movie theaters with fantasies of romantic love which they hoped would become reality. These daydreams carried over into their daily lives, creating unfulfilled longings which became obsessions. They replayed love scenes in their minds, over and over, with themselves as the leading ladies in the arms of handsome heroes. These love scenes were idealized and romanticized, devoid of explicit sexuality. The daydreams reflected what they had seen on the screen—long, soulful gazes into the lover's eyes, deep kisses, and a magical melting into each other's arms as the scene fades away, leaving the rest to the imagination. They truly believed that with the right man, they would experience continuous romantic ecstasy.

They lived in a world of unreality, in a never-never land. Rather than picturing sweat, smells, and secretions of the genitalia, they just saw more and more kissing and more and more melting into euphoria. They carried these delicious obsessions into their daily routines, using them to escape their mundane and unexciting lives, just as today's women dream of chocolate eclairs and truffles to escape their humdrum lives.

Women's obsessions with romance were further titillated by countless magazine stories which described in euphemistic romantic language the ecstacy of being in love and lovemaking, which were inseparable, especially for the impressionable female reader who had little or no factual sexual knowledge and had never seen either her genitals or a man's. Magazines such as "True Story," "True Confessions," "True Love," and "True Romance" were furtively read under the bedcovers and surreptitiously hidden between other reading material. Women consumed the stories in these magazines like one would devour a box of chocolates.

"I remember hiding the magazines way under the bed," said Maxine, a woman who went to high school and got married in the 1950s, "and then when the house was quiet, I furtively retrieved them. I would slip under the covers with my flashlight and excitedly devour the words on the page. I can recall feeling the physical sensations of sexual excitement as I identified with the passion and desire of the women in the stories. Often, after reading a story,

I would imagine my boyfriend doing the same things to me, and my fantasy life would go on and on.''

The secrecy and forbiddenness of reading these stories only made them more exciting and that stimulated the sexual appetite. The sexual references were not explicit, but their very vagueness created an excitement, a sense of mystery and magic, and fueled the fires of sexual fantasies. Sexual appetites were aroused just by seeing the forbidden words on the pages, just as women's appetites are stimulated by seeing food images in print, and on TV, today.

SHARED SECRETS

The obsession with sex was reinforced and magnified as girls got together and shared both their romantic fantasies and sexual secrets. Maxine describes this time in her life:

''My girlfriends and I exchanged magazines, but most exciting were the books found in the libraries of our parents or in the homes of people for whom we babysat. I remember babysitting for the people across the street, a young couple who had a marriage manual which I read so excitedly that I couldn't concentrate on the words. My constant fear was that they would come home unexpectedly and catch me doing the forbidden. Each time I discovered something new about sexuality, I could hardly wait to share it with my girlfriend.

''We were all virgins in high school but talked weekly at our club meetings about what 'it' would be like. As I look back, I can remember being fearful of letting my friends know I had petted below the waist. What would they think of me? And for a long time, I kept this secret to myself. I felt different having this secret, and replayed the scenes of my indiscretions over and over in my mind, walking to school, in class, and before I fell asleep. I wanted to talk to my friends and share both the exhilaration and the fears, but I did not know with whom I could safely share my secret.

''However, I was really lucky, because one of the girls in the club, on the way home from school, revealed to me that she had 'gone all the way' with her boyfriend, and what a relief it was to have a confidante. I remember walking endlessly around the block, talking with her in the greatest detail about our experiences. In addition to talking about the physical sensations, we wondered and thought about marriage. We naturally assumed that if we had done these forbidden things with our boyfriends, then the next step would be to get married.

At the same time there was also a fear that someone would find out about our transgressions. I particularly feared getting caught, and then this fear was fueled by the terror of becoming pregnant. I remember one girl in our school—she was a senior when I was only a freshman—who did get pregnant. Her name was Nancy, and she was one of the most popular girls in the school. She was going steady with this very handsome guy whom everybody had a crush on, and then one day we heard that she dropped out of school. Everyone talked about it. I remember being fascinated by this. It was rumored that Nancy and her boyfriend would 'go all the way' in the bushes during lunch and recess breaks, and I was simply consumed with curiosity and excitement about what happened between them. On the one hand, I was fascinated by her sexual experimentation; on the other hand, I felt dread that something like that could happen to me, that I could lose my head in passion, just as she did.

"Being pregnant was about the worst thing that could happen. The fear of getting pregnant added an element of danger and forbiddenness to our sexual experimentation; I remember nights driving way out in the country with my boyfriend to our regular parking place, anticipating the pleasures ahead. On the way, at every red light, we would stop and kiss open-mouthed, bodies alive with delicious feelings and sensuality and expectation. It seemed like forever until we reached our secret place beneath the heavy branches of the old trees that would protect us and provide a safe haven for our endless desires. I remember being so turned on that I felt I could not wait for us to park and for him to take off my clothes. When he reached down and put his hand through my underpants, the excitement was so great I felt I could hardly stand it. But the pleasure of touch would alternately provoke thoughts of 'I have to stop this, I can't do this anymore,' with thoughts of 'Oh, my God, I don't want to stop.' The conflict was unbearable and it only made the sexual feelings more intense and overpowering.

"As I look back to that time, I realize that I was obsessed with sex. It occupied almost all of my waking thoughts. It was on my mind all the time. I guess what accounted for my preoccupation with sex was that it was something I wanted desperately, but it was mysteriously dangerous and forbidden to me. Because of this, it held a unique excitement, an allure and a desire that was overwhelming."

Maxine's obsession with sex is typical of young women who reached sexual maturity in the 1950s. The taboo nature of the subject, the general ignorance and romanticizing of it, and the serious consequences of losing control all served to make it a major preoccupation of women growing up at that time.

We have been told similar stories by women who came of age in the 1960s and 1970s; however, these would-be good girls represented a minority, now that women were better equipped with knowledge of, and access to, birth control methods. "I remember the first time I heard about sex," said Louise, who grew up in the 1950s. "I was about eleven when my girlfriend whispered about it to me. She told me that she had heard about it from her cousin who was quite a bit older than her and who was going to be married soon. She told me all the details about it in very hushed, excited tones. She said that the man inserted his penis inside the woman, and that it was supposed to be the most wonderful, pleasurable experience in the world. I recall being awed by what she said, and I wanted to find out everything about it. I recall in my early teens discussing it with my friends, each more ignorant than the other, trying to learn as much as we could about this wonderful, mysterious, forbidden experience. We would spend hours in our room talking about it, wondering what it would be like and sneaking countless magazines into our bedroom looking for clues about this unknown experience.

"Of course, we found no factual clues in magazines, and words like vagina and clitoris were never mentioned. We all wanted information, but there was nobody to ask. I recall many years later asking a married friend what it was like, and she wasn't very helpful. She said, 'It's like a sneeze. How can you describe a sneeze to someone who has never had one?' This only added to the sense of mystery and curiosity about the whole subject.

"My friends and I would fantasize and romanticize about what it would be like, and we secretly wondered about older girls whom we knew had done it. We expressed ourselves in euphemisms then, never saying words like penis or vagina. We would blush when we talked about 'his thing'. As we grew older, each one of us wondered about each other's experiences but closely guarded the truth about our own sexual adventures.

"I recall fantasizing a lot in those days, usually about some guys in high school who were several years ahead of me and definitely unattainable. I would spend hours picturing myself in their arms, and I would get very aroused and excited when I would have these thoughts.

"I would lay in bed and listen for hours on end to slow, romantic music, and I would get in tune with the music, enraptured by it and lost in my daydreams. Looking back, it wasn't genital sex I pictured when I lost myself in my fantasies. It was kissing and holding and losing myself in love.

"We were obsessed with men and sex. We never discussed what we were going to be when we grew up or current events. When we were younger, we discussed the various crushes we had, and as we grew older and started dating, we discussed the guys we were going out with and those we wanted to go out with. All of our energies were focused on men and sex."

GOOD GIRLS DON'T GO "ALL THE WAY"

Like many women of her generation, Louise did not go all the way. Fear bordering on terror about getting pregnant and losing her reputation kept her and others from succumbing to the ultimate sin. Just as the fictional Marjorie Morningstar took two years and 417 pages of indecision and conflict before she gave herself to Noel Airman in the 1955 best seller, women of that era spent their teenage years guiltily agonizing over the decision to lose their virginity.

Sex was the darkest and dirtiest, the most exciting and sought-after obsession of its time. Of all secrets, sex was the most shameful. "Although nobody ever talked about sex that I can recall," said Rita, "I always had the feeling that it was dirty and somehow bad. When I first got my period, my mother avoided my eyes and blushed as she told me that this was something to expect every month from now on. Without explanation, she quickly handed me a sanitary belt and a box of Kotex. I could see that she was very uncomfortable so I didn't ask for instructions on how to put them on. I hid in the bathroom and struggled with the elastic belt which would not stay in place and the napkin which threatened to come loose if not attached properly. I felt very embarrassed and ashamed and I instinctively knew that this was not a subject that I could talk about with anyone else. Now that I look back, there was a feeling of shame and secrecy associated with that part of my body. It never had a name.

"When I was thirteen, I discovered that if I touched myself down there or if I squeezed my legs together real tight, I would get a very delicious sensation. I knew that this was not right and that I shouldn't be doing it. Some nights I would do it a little more or insert my finger deeper than normal. I would always worry that someone would catch me. Don't ask me how I knew this was wrong—I just knew. I believed that I was the only one who was doing this, that I was bad, and that either God would punish me or I would somehow damage myself. The secrecy and mystery of what I was doing only seemed to increase the pleasure I felt.

"Now that I think about it, I felt exactly the same way many years later when my boyfriend would put his hands in my underpants and fondle me. I would feel awful. I was sure I was the only girl who allowed a guy to take such liberties. I would have died if any of my friends would have found out about this. We would make out in out-of-the-way places, but I always worried that someone could sneak up on us and find us in that position. The dangerousness of it all only served to make it more exciting. Sometimes I would get so hot I could hardly bear it. When I look back, sex was so much more exciting then."

Rita's fear of what her girlfriends would think of her if they knew was a very real one. She did not want to be one of "those" girls that everyone whispered about. Everyone knew that there were two kinds of girls—those that men slept with and those that they married. If you were not careful, you could end up in the former category. No one wanted to be the bad girl who was talked about. "The danger of losing your reputation was always there," added Rita, "because you never knew if the guy would tell anybody. I always worried that my old boyfriend would talk to my new one and that they would compare notes. Somehow it was okay to do this with one guy if you were in love, but if you did this with everyone, you were in trouble. Those kinds of girls had reputations. So all of this had to be kept very secret, and there was always the fear that your secret would be let out. The danger of all this was enough to drive you crazy, and I thought about it all the time. I always thought of wanting to do it and not wanting to do it, wanting it badly but being so very afraid. The conflict was unbearable.

"In my mind, I would go over and over our petting sessions, feeling again the physical sensations and fantasizing about them. Then I would be filled with terror and shame about what I was doing. I would simply have died if anyone ever found out."

"Doing 'things' with a boyfriend was bad enough, but you got irrevocably damaged if you succumbed to the heat of the passion. You were then burned beyond repair. Those were the days before the pill, and I constantly worried that I would get pregnant. Our method of birth control was Fred promising to take it out just before he came. Now that I look back, I was lucky I never got pregnant, but each month I would wait with anguish for my period to come, and if it was a few days late, I would alternate between constantly checking my underpants and taking very hot baths. I lived in constant terror. I didn't know what I would do if I got pregnant. Everyone would then know what I had done. The shame of that was more than I could bear.

"Looking back," said Rita, "I am sure that the main reason I married my first husband at age 19 was because I went to bed with him. In those days, you only had intercourse with men you married. Unfortunately, intercourse was a great disappointment and could not compare to the exhilaration I felt during the clandestine petting sessions. I never had an orgasm. Nothing prepared me for the realities of intercourse."

Rita, like many women of her generation, suffered the effects of repressed sexuality. The constant denial of sexual needs, coupled with ignorance, created an inability to let go and enjoy sex. After years of monitoring her desires, she had effectively learned to inhibit her natural sexual responsivity. In the process of not going all the way, she taught herself to put a lid on her orgasmic capabilities.

ANYTHING FOR LOVE

The myriad of feelings that sex carried with it in the 1950s left young women in a perpetual emotional turmoil and made sex foremost in their minds. There was an ever-present conflict about sex. Shame, guilt, and fear, on the one hand, alternated with excitement and exhilaration on the other—all within a climate of secrecy and mystery. Sex carried with it both chills and thrills, terror and titillation, much as food does today.

"Sometimes, I get so hot, I can hardly bear it." These words, spoken by women in the 1950s, sound remarkably like those we hear from women today who say, "Sometimes I get so hungry, I can hardly bear it." When all these women described the feelings associated with indulging their appetites, the emotions were the same: fear, guilt, and shame. Today's women eat secretly, hide food, and hate themselves for binging. They examine their bodies to see if their shame will be made public, just as their forebearers checked their underpants compulsively for signs that they were not pregnant.

The behaviors we see today and those that existed in the past are both expressions of the same underlying issue. We want to be loved but fear no one will love us if we do not conform to the current standard of lovability. We are afraid that if we satisfy our own desires, we will face a lifetime of isolation and loneliness.

The struggle to put their own needs first and be true to their inner desires while simultaneously developing a love relationship has always been a problem for women. If I take care of my "selfish" needs, will my partner still love me? For many women, the threat of a severed connection is more than just the loss of a relationship; it can also be perceived as a loss of identity or self. Some women become depressed when facing the loss of a relationship, feeling empty and hopeless when emotional ties are broken. The need for affiliation is so important that it is valued more than self-fulfillment. Women will sacrifice their own needs to ensure their lovability.

In the past, women repressed their sexual needs and practiced rigid control over their passions to remain pure, moral, and thus, marketable. The result, for large numbers, was the inability to experience orgasm. They had so diligently practiced self-control and repressed their sexual impulses that, when married, they were unable to "let go" and experience sexual fulfillment. They remained good girls.

Chapter 5

The Sexual Revolution

>...I began looking at the pictures. Indeed, there was a cunt just like mine, and another and another. By the time we had gone through several magazines together I had an idea of what women's genitals looked like. What a relief! In that one session I found out I wasn't deformed, funny looking or ugly ...I was normal, and as my lover said, actually beautiful.
>
> —Betty Dodson, *Liberating Masturbation*

It was not until the late 1960s and early 1970s, with the arrival of the feminist and sexual revolution, that sex lost some of its mystery. The revolution was part and parcel of the women's movement. In *The Feminine Mystique* (1962), Betty Friedan talked about the "problem that has no name" that was plaguing women and called attention to the increasing dissatisfaction that women were experiencing in their lives. Friedan validated women's awareness that a husband, three children, and a home in the suburbs were not enough, and gave them permission to pursue career goals. She encouraged women to reexamine their roles and seek individual fulfillment. In 1966, Friedan helped organize the National Organization for Women (NOW) which, at that time, was the first new feminist organization in almost fifty years. This gave rise to, among other things, consciousness-raising groups where women met to discuss their concerns. Through these groups they learned to challenge the social structures and attitudes that had molded their thinking from birth.

The feminist movement had a tremendous impact on women's thinking and behavior, even for women who did not participate in those groups. There was a fervor in the air, raising new hopes and expectations for women of all ages. The movement was the single most important influence on women in the twentieth century. It was responsible for scores of females pursuing careers and entering the work force. Women demanded equal opportunity in the job market and the freedom to control their own destinies rather than depend on a man to provide them with happiness.

IT'S O.K. TO TOUCH "DOWN THERE"

To control one's body is to control one's destiny, and the feminist movement encouraged women to take control over their reproductive lives. Women demanded and won the right to legalized abortion, to decide for themselves whether to give birth instead of letting fate decide for them. In Boston, a small discussion group of women formed to address feminist issues, which culminated in the 1971 publication of *Our Bodies, Ourselves*, the widely read book that opened women's eyes to the workings of their bodies. It gave women information about their anatomy, contraception, pregnancy, and abortion. The mystery and darkness surrounding their bodies and bodily functions were replaced by open, clinical, factual information. Clinics and self-help groups sprung up in which women learned to examine their genitals and explore their bodies. What was always referred to as "down there" now had a name, and what was once hidden under the mattress was open for everyone to see. Women no longer had to rely on their imagination for sexual knowledge; now they had graphic details to educate them.

The simultaneous revolution in birth control—especially the advent of the Pill—freed women from the fear and terror of unwanted pregnancies. Anatomy was no longer destiny; that is, women could now *choose* whether or not to have children. As they were gaining equality and freedom in other areas, women demanded sexual equality and freedom as well. They started questioning the notion of virginity and "preserving" themselves for marriage, now that the fear of pregnancy was no longer paramount. They learned to "own" their sexuality, and to enjoy it without feeling guilty. The link between virginity and wedlock that had forced many women into premature marriages was now broken.

Women who read *Our Bodies, Ourselves* learned that they had a right to pleasure, and they were given specific instructions on how to achieve that pleasure through masturbation. What was done furtively under the bedcovers could now be read about in explicit detail. The mystery surrounding sexuality was replaced with factual knowledge. Women were excited about exploring their bodies and learning about their anatomy. "Although I still had a reservoir of guilt about looking at my body, it was so liberating to take a mirror and look at my genitals for the first time. I had an exhilarated feeling when I found my clitoris and touched it without shame," said one woman. Comments like this were frequent in consciousness-raising and self-help groups, where women were encouraged to take charge of their bodies.

Sex, previously seen only in mystical and magical terms, now became an object of scientific study. In St. Louis, Missouri, hundreds of people volunteered to be observed and monitored in a laboratory while engaged in sexual activity. The research team headed by William H. Masters, M.D., and Virginia E. Johnson broke daring new ground by studying sexual behavior, going so far as to place instruments on subjects' genitals to measure physiological changes taking place throughout the human sexual response cycle. They took pictures and films to graphically depict all the bodily changes during an orgasm. They could even tell to the tenth of a second how many contractions occurred with each climax. The romantic, illusive sexual experience was now dissected, analyzed, and quantified in a sterile, clinical environment.

Human sexuality courses sprang up in universities and colleges all across the country. Students flocked to these courses in increasing numbers. Textbooks and paperbacks on sexuality came rolling off the presses, dispensing sexual information to anyone who sought it. What had been private, discussed only in whispers behind closed doors, became the object of open discussion in classrooms. Students watched films of people engaging in all types of sexual activity, in order to become "desensitized" from guilt-ridden inhibitions. Sex was taken out of the closet in medical schools as well. Medical students watched movies of couples making love with the same detached and analytical attitude they applied to the observation of surgical films. The glamour and mystery surrounding sex was gone. Technical terms replaced all the titillating euphemisms describing male and female anatomy.

DEBUNKING SEXUAL MYTHS

The application of scientific principles to the study of human sexuality resulted in new methods for the treatment of sexual problems. Whereas in the past, a woman's inability to experience an orgasm was believed to be a result of her immaturity and was treated by long-term psychoanalysis, she could now be helped by the new sex therapy methods which Masters and Johnson developed, based on their laboratory observations.

Masters and Johnson's research findings made headline news and debunked many of the myths about female sexuality, the biggest one being the vaginal orgasm. It was believed at the time that there were two kinds of orgasms—vaginal and clitoral—with the vaginal being the "real thing," the one that counted. Having an orgasm through intercourse was the "right" way to do it. Only "mature" women were presumed to have vaginal orgasms, and their counterparts who experienced clitoral orgasms were considered neurotic and emotionally immature. The laboratory findings, that there was only one kind of orgasm and its source was in the clitoris, refuted these widely held beliefs.

Masters and Johnson debunked another myth of human sexuality: sexual intercourse in the standard missionary position did *not* automatically result in sexual satisfaction for the woman because the clitoris was not directly stimulated. Intense sexual satisfaction did not result from vaginal penetration, but from clitoral stimulation.

Masters and Johnson offered treatment for men and women who were experiencing sexual difficulties, offering an intense two-week treatment program with nightly homework assignments designed to *teach* patients how to make love. They had very dramatic positive results and made sex a teachable skill devoid of mystical qualities. Masters and Johnson made their knowledge public, training therapists all across the country in their methods. Education, communication, and sexual exercises replaced the ignorance and misinformation surrounding sexuality.

LIBERATING ORGASM

One very influential therapist at that time was Lonnie Barbach whose book, *For Yourself: The Fulfillment of Female Sexuality* (1975), was read by millions of women. Barbach encouraged women to take charge of their own sexuality, to take matters into their own hands, so to speak. She developed a systematic masturbation program to teach women to have orgasms. Women met in groups to discuss sexuality, and were given homework assignments to touch and explore their bodies. These groups were called preorgasmic women's groups because Barbach believed that women could become orgasmic by learning how to masturbate. This, in fact, was the case, as over 90 percent of the women participating in these groups were able to achieve orgasm. Through these groups, women learned not only to be sexually assertive but also to transfer this assertiveness to other areas of their lives. While learning to appreciate their bodies and derive pleasure from them, their feelings of self-worth and well-being increased. Women realized they had a right to sexual pleasure and began taking more responsibility for their own sexual satisfaction. As they became more comfortable in communicating their likes and dislikes, they were able to achieve sexual satisfaction.

Barbach's influence on women's sexuality was far reaching. Millions of women read her book and used her methods to become orgasmic. What had been hidden and dirty was now openly described and portrayed in positive terms. What was taboo and mysterious was now explained in clear language.

Barbach essentially allowed women to see themselves as sexual beings and to be sexual, telling them they were not "bad girls" for having sexual feelings. The forbidden was now permissible; in fact, it was *expected*. Women could expect to have an orgasm with each sexual encounter, and when they learned that they were capable of having more than one orgasm, their expectations soared. Many women prided themselves on being multi-orgasmic.

Barbach's message also reached the professional community. Psychiatrists, psychologists, and therapists from all over the country flocked to her workshops to be trained in her methods so that they could go back to their communities and start preorgasmic women's groups. Therapists learned rather straightforward, simple techniques which every woman could master if she put the time and effort into it. They taught their clients that having an orgasm was not a mysterious phenomenon, but a physiological response that could be learned through education, self-exploration, and practice.

As therapists trained by Barbach, we can remember the excitement of the women in our groups who experienced orgasms for the first time. A whole new world was opening to them. One woman was so ecstatic over her first orgasm that she and her husband cried tears of joy: they had discovered a new level of intimacy. Other women were proud of the fact that they could now control their bodies. That they could take charge of their bodies gave them permission to take charge of other aspects of their lives. "If I can give myself an orgasm, I can do anything," said one housewife, who later went to law school and became an attorney.

THE SEXUAL LIBERTY BELL IS RINGING

The message that women had a right to, and were responsible for, their own sexual pleasure was spread during the 1970s by others, such as Betty Dodson in her booklet *Liberating Masturbation*, and Nancy Friday in *My Secret Garden* and *Forbidden Flowers*. Barbach, Dodson and Friday were all part of the sexual revolution sweeping America, a revolution that was buoyed along by a new openness in all the media. Right on prime time television, "Maude" (Bea Arthur) had the audacity to declare that she was going to have an abortion, something which was unthinkable in the previous decade. Loretta Lynn, the famous country singer, released a song called "The Pill" which hinted at the woman's new freedom to engage in extramarital affairs, just as her husband did. Erica Jong's 1973 novel, *Fear of Flying*, introduced a sexually assertive heroine, and the fantasy of the "zipless fuck." Jong portrayed women as having the same desires, fantasies, and experiences as men. A number of how-to books on sexuality came out in this era: *Everything You Always Wanted To Know About Sex But Were Afraid To Ask* (Reuben, 1970), *The Sensuous Man* ("M," 1972), *The Sensuous Woman* ("J," 1971) and *The Sensuous Couple* (Chartham, 1987).

Films also began to show a new openness about sex. Couples no longer made love only from the neck up, and nudity and the use of four-letter words were so commonplace as to be routine. Abortions, homosexuality, and extramarital sex were depicted on the screen without too much ado.

The sexual revolution even reached the halls of ivy: Dr. Lester Kirkendall, noted sexologist and Professor of Family Life at the University of Oregon, drafted what was to become a "New Bill of Sexual Rights and Responsibilities," endorsed by some of the leading humanists of the time. Sexuality was now considered a moral responsibility. The bill of rights (1977-1978) declared that each person has both an *obligation* and a *right* to be fully informed about sexuality, and that physical pleasure has worth as a *moral* value. The bill condemned traditional views of sexuality as "wicked" or "sinful," stating that these attitudes were inhumane and destructive of relationships. It stated that the deprivation of pleasure contributed to family breakdowns, child abuse, crime, violence, and other forms of dehumanizing behavior. Physical pleasure was seen as *essential*.

The sexual revolution was truly a revolution, with its own bill of rights, slogans, and sayings. Thousands of middle class people joined the movement, shedding their old conservative uniforms for blue jeans, long hair, and a "hang loose" attitude. Women were "natural" and "free," braless and barefoot. They were encouraged to go back to their natural, primitive urges, and what could be more natural and primitive than sex? Hot tubs and water beds could be found in many middle class homes, and sexual experimentation became the thing to do. Swinging and open marriages were legitimized under the guise of "doing one's own thing." Getting rid of inhibitions was the name of the game, and promiscuity became commonplace. For the more adventuresome, sexual weekends were available, where people could go by themselves or as a couple, and have sex with whomever pleased them. Nobody wanted to be thought of as "uptight" about sex.

Young girls could not wait to get rid of their virginity, which was now considered a burden instead of a blessing. A 25-year-old single woman could be just as embarrassed to admit that she was a virgin as her mother would have been to admit that she was not. Premarital sex was now expected, and couples started living together openly.

Interestingly, women seem to be "doing it" at younger and younger ages through the generations, paralleling the cases of eating disorders, which seem to be afflicting younger and younger women— even pre-teens. Today's young girls are more embarrassed about being fat than about not being virgins. Although loss of virginity ceased to bring shame, women still worried about becoming pregnant, in spite of the Pill and more readily available birth control methods. In 1973, the Supreme Court legalized abortion in the United States, giving women further control over their bodies by guaranteeing their right to terminate an unwanted pregnancy in a safe and professional manner, avoiding one consequence of being sexually active.

CASUAL SEX AND ONE NIGHT STANDS

The sexual revolution marked an extraordinary sharp break with traditionally held values. A woman who married in the late 1950s and found herself divorced a decade later was in for a rude awakening. Prior to her marriage, she had limited her sexual activity, but now, as a single woman again, she was expected to have a more casual attitude about sex. What was before reserved for the marital relationship became the norm of dating behavior. Casual sex and one-night stands became common occurrences.

For many, it was difficult to reconcile old attitudes with current expectations. Many women still felt guilty after one-night stands, even though they were supposed to be "liberated" from the old sexual inhibitions. Many could not let go of their old beliefs and attitudes and were still sensitive to society's condemnation of the "free" woman. These women still had to rationalize that they were carried away by passion in order to feel guilt-free about being sexual. Carol Cassell, in her book *Swept Away: Why Women Fear Their Own Sexuality* (1984), describes the phenomenon of being "Swept Away" as a coping mechanism which allows women to be sexual in a society that is still ambivalent and sometimes condemnatory of female sexuality. To avoid being labeled wanton or promiscuous, many women become Swept Away to disguise their own erotic desires.

The sexual revolution had a profound effect on women's sexual behavior. What had been repressed and forbidden became open and encouraged, and what had been mysterious and romantic became casual and commonplace. Sex was no longer tied to love and commitment. Now that it was readily available, it was no longer an obsession. Women no longer needed to think the unthinkable or fantasize about a day far in the future when they could consummate their passion—they could now go into any singles bar and act out their fantasies. Sexual satisfaction was their *right!*

Now that women were freed from their sexual obsessions, they could shift their attention elsewhere. It was not long after the sexual revolution that we began to see the first signs of disinterest in sex. When we first practiced sex therapy, we saw literally hundreds of women obsessed with the need for sexual fulfillment: they wanted the perfect sexual experience. Ten years later, almost all the women we see talk about a periodic lack of desire. Many have no idea why they have no interest in sex. Oh yes, they can have an orgasm, but so what? Women today are more focused on success, competing in their careers, making money—and on being *somebody*.

Chapter 6

Sex: More Trouble Than It's Worth

As these magazine covers tell us, women are thinking up ways to rekindle their sex lives.

Don't let marriage ruin your love life.
—Redbook (December 1988)

"Not tonight; I have a headache" has become "Not this year; I have a career."
—Asa Baber, *Playboy* (March 1987)

How to put passion back in your relationship
—New Woman (October 1985)

Too Tired and Tense for Sex? 12 Aphrodisiacs That Work!
—Redbook (July 1990)

Does sex appeal to women?
—Mademoiselle (June 1985)

Why have women lost interest in sex? Is it possible that women are turning away from relationships? Are romance, sensuality, and sexuality slipping down from first place?

Women are focusing on themselves, particularly on what and how much they put into their mouths, and how often they do so. They spend their time thinking about food, about what to eat, and what not to eat. They are obsessed with the body beautiful, with being in shape. They think about the number of calories they consume and know how many calories are in a hard-boiled egg.

In today's era of disappointing relationships, many women are turning inward for their sources of gratification. In their fast-paced world with multiple demands, they are looking for something that requires little from them. They seek relief from their stress and turn to food to fulfill an inner emptiness. Food is the ideal lover—it is impersonal, nondemanding, easily attainable, and instantly gratifying. It provides physical satisfaction without many of the new dreaded consequences of casual sex.

Yoko came for therapy because she was not interested in having sex. Once a week was fine for her (though even once was a chore, because she was never in the mood) but her husband wanted to have sex three times a week. Yoko had a two-year-old child, a home to take care of, clothes to wash and iron, and meals to prepare. She also wanted to be a successful career woman because she felt it was more an expression of herself than being attached to a man. She found fulfillment not in bed but in the marketplace.

She was working very hard to build her business, and it occupied her thoughts at home and at work. If she did not have her business, she would be forced to be a secretary and would have to take orders from some man. This was her opportunity to be free, creative, financially independent, and fulfilled—to be the picture of success. That picture required her to watch what she eats, to carefully count her calories, and to limit the amount of sugar and fat in her diet. The successful career woman has to be slim and well dressed, for her self-esteem depends on it. And her success, in turn, depends on her self-esteem.

THE NUMBER ONE COMPLAINT: LACK OF SEXUAL DESIRE

Yoko's problem is not unusual. Lack of desire is the sexual complaint most reported to therapists. In Dr. Helen Singer Kaplan's *Disorders of Sexual Desire* (1979), she defines these disorders as follows: "A person has no interest in erotic matters; he 'loses his appetite' for sex and becomes 'asexual.' Pleasure is fleeting, perhaps just before orgasm, and is limited to or localized in the genitals. Patients describe such experiences as similar to eating a meal when one is not really hungry."

"Inhibited sexual desire" has become so pronounced that it is now an official diagnostic entity, considered a sexual dysfunction in the American Psychiatric Association's *Diagnostic and Statistical*

Manual (1980). Carol Botwin, in her book *Is There Sex After Marriage?* (1985), discusses the parameters of this problem. Some therapists have estimated that half of their patients are turned off to sex. In addition, several surveys have shown that infrequent sex is very common in marriage. In a survey of 100 married couples, one-third reported having intercourse two or three times a month or less. In another survey, a third had not had sex for longer periods of time. Some couples had gone without intercourse for over three months.

Masters, Johnson, and Kolodny address this phenomenon in their book *Masters and Johnson on Sex and Human Loving* (1982), a nearly 700-page volume discussing all the changes since the sexual revolution. Although sex today is ever-present and far more accessible, the authors reveal a general dissatisfaction with sex which is unusual in the midst of near total sexual freedom. They report that half of all U.S. marriages are troubled by some form of sexual distress, ranging from disinterest and boredom to outright sexual dysfunction.

Even more disturbing is the lack of desire that occurs in younger couples. Botwin summarizes the results of a recent study: "...more than three-quarters of the husbands and wives making do with little or no sex were under the age of thirty-eight—a prime time in life, when intercourse between spouses, on an average, takes place two or three times a week."

Probably one of the most publicized surveys of women's attitudes toward sexual intercourse was conducted by Ann Landers. When Ann Landers (1985) asked her readers, "Would you be content to be held close and treated tenderly and forget about the act?", 72 percent of the 90,000 women surveyed said yes. Of those 72 percent, 40 percent were under 40 years of age.

SEX: ONE MORE DEMAND

The lack of passion is most pronounced in the two-paycheck family. Picture this scene: at the completion of a long working day, she sits in the living room looking at her briefcase full of paperwork, and he is sprawled across the couch watching television. Both husband and wife are zonked out. They are too tired for sex, and even if they had the energy, they would probably have no time for it. This scenario is played in varying degrees by many two-career couples. At the end of a hectic day, they usually find themselves drained, and their workday is still not over. There are meals to prepare, after-dinner cleanup, errands to run and sometimes children to put to bed. The constant demands on their time and energy leave very little room for sex.

Claire and Tom are an example of a modern career couple whose interest in sex has had a dramatic decline. They are both attractive physicians in their early thirties who love each other very much, but have intercourse on the average of once a month. "I can't understand it," said Claire, a vivacious, beautiful woman whose frustration was noted in her speech. "At the beginning of our rela-tionship, we just couldn't keep our hands off each other. We always did romantic things for each other, bought expensive gifts and could never get enough of each other. But now I feel like I am only a part of the furniture. I would like him to see me as a lover, as someone special. I know he loves me, and I love him, but we seem to be like two girlfriends. I want to get that special feeling again." Claire sighed and continued, "It's not as though we have neglected each other. I have seen too many couples put their careers above their relationships, and Tom and I tried not to make the mistake so we invested most of our energy on each other. I didn't get married until I was thirty, and I really don't care that much for my career. I have always wanted to be a wife and mother. Yet my work still takes much of my time and energy, and now that we have a baby whom we both adore, that takes up even more time. Usually we just plop into bed near each other without even thinking about sex. I know there is something wrong because we are both young, only in our thirties. Two people like us who are still in love with each other should have sex more than once a month, shouldn't they?"

Unfortunately, Claire and Tom's situation is becoming more commonplace, even among couples who love each other and have rewarding, pleasurable sexual experiences together. Even when couples make a conscious effort to preserve the romance in their lives, as Claire and Tom did, other demands absorb their energies, leaving little desire or inclination for sex. Claire's work-related stress inter-fered with her sexual drive, even though she placed a *lower* priority on her work than on her home life. As Carol Botwin (1985) states:

> Although work-related stress is very common in our culture, people rarely realize how much it can dampen their sex lives. A new boss, a promotion, or transfer, a job insecurity, or unemployment can make a person practically oblivious to sex.... (p. 194)

In women for whom career success *is* a priority, lack of sexual desire is even more prevalent. Virginia entered therapy at her husband's insistence. She is a thin, attractive, energetic woman in her late twenties who was intent on having a productive career. Two years ago, after the birth of her first child, she quit a boring secretarial position. However, she was depressed staying at home and decided to get a real estate license, eventually landing a job with a high-powered real estate company. To be available to clients, Virginia had to put in long hours, including evenings and weekends. In addition, she had to always look thin and fashionable. "I love my husband," Virginia began. "I don't want a divorce, but I am never in the mood for sex. I don't care if I ever have sex again. I don't know what has happened to me. I find ways of avoiding my husband's advances. The few times we do have sex, I enjoy it and can have orgasms, but there is a block whenever he touches me. I have no desire, and sex is never on my mind. I know I should want it, but I don't."

Virginia, like many ambitious superwomen, tried to do it all. In addition to a demanding career, she felt a need to cook a nutritional dinner for her family every night and keep an immaculate house. Moreover, her desire to present a thin and attractive professional image meant going to the health spa at least twice a week. "I crawl into bed exhausted," she said, "and all I want to do is go to sleep. The last thing I want to do at night is make love." Virginia viewed sex as one more demand on her already overloaded schedule.

Like many superwomen, Virginia was very angry at her husband for his lack of responsibility in sharing household tasks, and this anger intensified the lack of desire for sex. As Marjorie Hansen Shaevitz states in *The Superwoman Syndrome* (1984): "I find that sexual aversiveness, as opposed to other kinds of sexual problems, occurs more frequently in couples in which the wife is a Superwoman. A combination of fatigue, unexpressed anger, and lack of effective communication is often at the core.'' When exhaustion from stress is causing lack of sexual desire, sex if often seen as still another chore. Dr. Herbert Freudenberger and Gail North, in their book *Woman's Burnout* (1985), say career women are trying to keep up with too many role demands. In addition to a general feeling of detachment and exhaustion, the fire of sexual feeling seems gone, with sexual intercourse being seen as just another demand or chore. This is such a far cry from the 1950s, when sex was a primary obsession.

THE SINGLE WOMAN: WHERE DO I FIT SEX INTO MY LIFE?

The single career woman has even more complicated sexual issues to deal with than her married counterpart. Just like her married sister, she is finding career demands all-consuming, and she does not have the energy required to build a new relationship. Also, in spite of the sexual revolution, she is still plagued with doubts about how sexually active she should be. Her doubts and fears are increased because sexual activity may result in one of the numerous sexually transmitted diseases. She begins to think that devoting her energies to her career will be more rewarding than having a lover who may ultimately leave her with herpes, VD or AIDS. Is it any wonder then, that for many single women, sex seems more trouble than it is worth? It is not surprising that so many women today are choosing celibacy.

This declining interest in sex for single women is even more striking when viewed against the background of their sexual freedom. In the first government survey to assess the sexual habits of single women between the ages of 19 and 30, it was found that unmarried women in their twenties have had sexual relations, on the average, with 4.5 men, half of whom were long-term boyfriends, and the other half, casual acquaintances. One-third of the women surveyed have lived with a man whom they never wed, and a third of them have been pregnant. Clearly, premarital sex, cohabitation, and out-of-wedlock pregnancies are very common in single women today. Yet, in spite of the casual nature sex has assumed, and maybe because of it, many single women consider it more trouble than it is worth.

"It's just not worth it," said Patricia, a successful attorney, when asked why she was not in a relationship. "Sure, I'd love to have someone love me and be there for me. Who wouldn't? But it's such a hassle. I hate to play the games necessary to get to know someone, and the meat markets and the bar scene completely turn me off. Two years ago, I lived with a man whom I loved very much, but the day-to-day struggle of keeping up a relationship got to be too much work. I couldn't come home and crawl into bed with a good book. I had to talk to him, get his dinner ready and be a companion for him. There was no time for me. He used to travel a lot for his job, and I hate to admit this, but I used to look forward to those times when I could relax and be by myself. I didn't worry then about working late or bringing work home or talking on the telephone with my girlfriends. Maybe some day in the future I will have a relationship, but right now it is too much of a hassle. Frankly, I'd rather come home to a good book, a glass of wine, and a pizza."

Several authors have recognized the problem of single women who are choosing careers over sexual relationships. Megan Marshall addresses this problem in her book *The Cost of Loving* (1984), in which she describes interviews with women who were "revelling in new feelings of power and competence" and did not let men or sex interfere with these feelings. The cost of loving, of being sexual, was too great. In their book *Too Smart for Her Own Good?* (1985), psychologists Conalee Levine-Shneidman and Karen Levine also discuss how many career women, inordinately fearful of losing their hard-won emotional and economic independence, repress their nurturing instincts and avoid sexual relationships. Psychologist Srully Blotnick, author of *Otherwise Engaged* (1985), asserts that career women have sacrificed their personal lives because of their ambition. This craving to excel in a career has driven thousands of women into the business world where they have turned themselves into what he terms "toughies" who have repressed their nurturing instincts and "prudes" who are sexually repressed.

Recently, a therapist told us of her frustration in attempting to have a live-in sexual partner: "Last night I was too tired and exhausted to make love, and he became angry and irritated with me. I had spent the last few days shopping and cooking for the holidays, in addition to working overtime and seeing people who were coping with holiday stress. And I just got furious with him, and I started screaming and yelling. I hate myself for getting out of control. Doesn't he realize how much I have to do? I love sex. That's probably one reason I stay with him, but is it worth this?''

For the career woman who is divorced and also has children, finding time for sex and romance can be something of an achievement. The logistics of fitting a sexual relationship into her life while juggling babysitters, ex-husbands, and lovers, are compounded by the additional worry of how her sexual relations will affect her children. Single mothers still like to maintain a certain image in front of their children, to set a good example. Should the man sleep in? Should he come to live with them? Having a sexual relationship can be more than a minor undertaking for divorced women. One of our friends, a divorcee with two small children, said, ''Sex will just have to wait until my children grow up. It takes all the energy I have to work to support them, and what little time I have left, I want to spend with them. I just don't have the time for sex anymore. It's just not worth it.''

Over and over, we hear the same words: It's not worth it. Women are weighing the direction of their lives and deciding where to put their energies. For many women, a career offers prestige, power, status, independence, excitement, as well as monetary rewards—a career means an identity. And many women find their autonomy and identity slipping away when they merge with a man. For them, the price is too high, and these women have eliminated men and sex from their lives.

For many of these women, food has become their lover. Food makes no demands on their time, it provides comfort *and* it is readily available. When they go to the refrigerator to find satisfaction, they do not have to worry about maintaining an image in front of their children. They do not have to deal with the hassle of getting the man out of their bed before dawn. Food, unlike sex, offers instant gratification and requires no commitment.

A GOOD MAN IS HARD TO FIND

Many other women are *not* willing to give up men. They are actively pursuing career goals while hunting for a husband. The mating game is a considerably more serious undertaking than it was many years ago. Fred Moody describes "Love After 30," (*L.A. Weekly*, June 21-27, 1985), as a slow painful shuffle involving a great deal of hard work. A woman back in the dating game after six years of a long, steady relationship finds a sense of urgency about commitment now. People are desperate, lonely, and long to be married. "And the 1970's stuff—the 'love the one you're with' attitude—seems to be gone. Dates are more marriage-oriented now," he observes. In their desperation, women are viewing every man as a potential husband. There is no room for spontaneity. For many women, trying to fall in love according to a plan can be very hard work.

Barbara Bottner's words give a flavor of this singles' mentality in the same issue of the *L.A. Weekly:*

> Lonely. Will go to the party. (You never know.) Get dressed: flat shoes, be comfortable. After all, you still have a touch of fever. Can't do it. Can't wear flat shoes, won't be sexy enough. Put on the high heels, the highest you own. Okay. Better... You'd like to meet somebody. Really, it's time already. You're in the outer limits of your outer 30's...

The desperation inherent in the above passage becomes intensified because there are many more single women than single men. For example, in Los Angeles, the ratio of marriage-available men to marriage-available women decreases as the woman grows older. If a woman is between 25 and 29, she has the best chance to find a mate because there are 97 single men for every 100 single women. When she crosses the threshold into her thirties, the odds of finding a husband are decreased, as there are only 82 available men for every 100 women between the ages of 30 and 34. If she has not found a mate by age 35, her chances become even slimmer. There are only 65 potential mates for every 100 women between the ages of 35 and 40. This means that there are only two males for every three single females. After 45, the chances are almost nil—about one in a hundred.

A recent highly publicized study is more pessimistic about the chances for single women to find Prince Charming. The covers of *People* magazine (March 31, 1986) and *Newsweek* (June 2, 1986) literally scream out the findings of this study and tell you that if you are over 35 and single, you can forget about getting married (Levir, 1986; Kantrowitz, Witherspoon, Williams, King, 1986). According to the report by two Yale psychologists and a Harvard economist, white, college-educated women who are still single at 30 have only a 20 percent chance of marrying. By age 35, their chances drop to 5 percent. If they turn 40 and are still single, their chances of getting married are only 2.6 percent. Even though the results of this study have been refuted to some extent, these findings still bring panic and despair to single women.

Not only is there a numerical scarcity of eligible men, but of the remaining available bachelors, many are scared of commitment. They wrestle with fears of entrapment and bolt when the subject of marriage comes up. Many of these men are wary of marriage, having been hurt in previous relationships. They are afraid of making commitments and live a life of protracted bachelorhood. As many women tell us, "All the men we know are either married, gay, or confirmed bachelors." A good man is hard to find, and many women are faced with the prospect of being alone. Is it any wonder they turn to food?

For some women, the anxiety about being alone can lead to compulsive overeating. They eat out of loneliness and despair, and because the food is there and inviting. They eat out of boredom, and they eat out of anger. For a few brief moments, the food quells their anxiety. But food as a lover is a double-edged sword because at the same time that it provides comfort, it creates new problems. It keeps them from remaining slim and attractive and lowers their chances of attracting one of the few marriageable men.

THE MECHANIZATION OF ROMANCE

The ticking biological clock and the dismal male-female ratio pressure the single woman over thirty to seek a mate, but finding one and fitting him into her already busy life is very difficult. The single woman is usually not in situations where she is likely to meet single men. In addition, she does not want to invest her precious time going to churches, social clubs, or gatherings just on the off-chance that an eligible man will present himself. Many women have turned to professional dating services with computer-powered equipment to find a suitable man.

Most cities have several matchmaking services, some of which are exclusively designed for well-educated career singles. Pressured single women will pay large fees, $200 to $2,000, for an introduction to a possible marriage partner. The romance of a chance meeting is replaced by the efficiency of a computer-selected partner. Computerized matchmaking services, once considered the last resort for the socially inept, are now a recognized method for meeting people. Thus, single women approach their personal goals in the same organized, efficient manner with which they approach their professional goals, so that establishing a loving partnership is like work. The fires of mystery and romance that once fueled sexual relationships have become mechanized and computerized.

A successful attorney talked about her experience with a local dating service. Gloria is a 36-year-old divorced woman with a stunning figure and a very attractive face. She is bright, vivacious, and has no difficulty attracting men. "At this time in my life," she said, "I have no time to waste because I am thirty-six and want to have a child. I have to meet a man who will be a good husband and father, so I joined this dating service where I get at least two introductions a week. First I meet them for a drink, and then I decide if I want to invest anymore time with them. I have no time to invest my energy in a relationship that is not going anywhere. At first, I was uneasy and suspicious of dating services, but now I make it a point of blanking out my appointment book two nights a week for new introductions."

Gloria uses the dating service much as one uses a consultant to solve business problems. Twice weekly, introductions are scheduled like everything else in her appointment book, and she screens her marital applicants with the same efficiency with which one screens a job applicant. The businesslike quality of these meetings is a far cry from the mystery and uncertainty of a romantic encounter, a sharp contrast to the love and romance of the 1950s.

"Since I made up my mind to get married and have a child, I have had to cut back on my work schedule and to re-assess my career goals," continued Gloria. "If I want to meet someone and have a relationship, I need to make time to do it." For women like Gloria, trying to make room for a potential relationship in an already busy calendar can be a difficult task. By the time a woman is in her mid-thirties, she has already established a network of friends and set routines. The chances are that her dating partner will have career and social demands of his own. Their love life can evolve into a series of scheduled appointments, and the spontaneity which is characteristic of beginning love affairs disappears. Time for lovemaking is carefully pencilled into its allotted space in the little black book.

In addition, many women today see a man as an extension of themselves and are afraid that others will judge them as imperfect if they marry someone who is not particularly good-looking or successful. They work very hard at finding a mate of whom they can be proud. The chore of pursuing the perfect man detracts from their feelings, resulting in detachment and superficiality in sexual relationships. The act of sex becomes mechanical, performance-oriented, and devoid of feelings, part of the goal-oriented program to get a partner, rather than an act of love and intimacy. Intimacy requires exposing vulnerabilities and imperfections to a partner, but this is impossible in an atmosphere of self-conscious perfectionism.

The mechanization of love today is a far cry from the "sweet mystery of love" of yesteryear, with its romantic songs, films, and fantasies. There is no more anticipation, mystery, or titillation—this has given way to guardedness, cynicism, and stark realism. The magic of finding Prince Charming across a crowded room has been replaced by software and a print-out.

IS IT WORTH DYING FOR?

Another problem that can keep women from entering into and enjoying a sexual relationship is the risk of contracting sexually transmitted diseases. Erica Jong describes this state of affairs in her book *Parachutes and Kisses* (1984) when she writes about her modern, sexually liberated heroine's plight:

Ought she to worry about clap?...Or was it herpes you were supposed to worry about these days? Things had changed so drastically since her adolescence that she hardly knew *what* to worry about! In *her* adolescence in the 1950s, pregnancy was the big worry, the big P...

For some women, sex is so fraught with complications that they may decide to forego it altogether. "I have a phobia about getting AIDS," said Jessica, a young woman who had recently separated from her husband. "I don't love my husband and don't find him sexually appealing at all, but at least with him I'm safe. I would really like to leave him and find someone who really turns me on, but sometimes I think I should just stay with him because I am so afraid of catching something."

Several months ago, one of our clients called. She sounded hysterical and was sobbing. "I am absolutely freaking out," she said between sobs. "I couldn't sleep all night. My boyfriend just told me he had an outbreak of herpes when we had intercourse, and there is a good chance I may have it. I am going out of my mind with worry because I won't get the test results back for a week, and I don't know whether I have it or not." The consequences of having herpes go beyond the physical manifestations of blisters and flu-like symptoms. Although these symptoms may only appear a couple of times a year, it is the stigma associated with a sexually transmitted disease that creates the strong negative emotional response. As one woman said, "That's a *dirty* disease. I can't believe that *I* could get it. Nice girls like me don't get herpes." The stigma carries with it a terrible shame, so that people with herpes are embarrassed to tell anyone about their illness and begin to feel like outcasts or lepers.

Many women with herpes do not venture out at all, becoming social isolates and avoiding contact with men that could lead to romantic involvement. The agony of how to tell, when to tell, and the real risk of rejection become more painful than being alone. The despair and hopelessness that women feel when they learn that they have herpes is compounded by the fact that it is incurable and that they can be plagued with outbreaks at any time. As one woman said, "I'm sure God is punishing me." The possibility of contracting herpes and other venereal diseases has contributed to women becoming more cautious in their sexual behavior.

More prevalent than herpes but curable with antibiotics is gonor-rhea. The reported incidence of gonorrhea has increased by 15 percent in the past decade. Although exact numbers are not known since many people do not report that they have a venereal disease, it is estimated that there are about two or three million new cases of gonor-rhea in the United States every year. The chance of being infected is quite high if one has many sex partners. Gonorrhea can cause infertility in women if the infection spreads to the fallopian tubes.

Of all the sexually transmitted diseases, the most devastating one is AIDS. The thought of contracting this deadly disease strikes terror in the hearts of most single women. In a very short period of time, AIDS has evolved from a relatively unheard of virus to the most dreaded disease of the decade. There is a mass hysteria generated by the fear of becoming a victim of this illness. Women who have had multiple sexual partners are going in droves to get tested for the AIDS virus. Many women are so worried that they get tested more than once. Nowadays when women have sex, they do not worry so much whether they will have an orgasm or get pregnant, they are more worried that they will literally *die!*

Because women are much more cautious about their sexual behavior today, they are much less likely to go to bed with someone because they are horny or lonely. They frequently ask their dates to wear condoms and are reluctant to go to bed at all with someone whose sexual history is in doubt. Women say that they can no longer engage in spontaneous sex. They have to screen out their partners, carry condoms, and still take a chance on their health. AIDS has taken much of the fun out of their sex lives.

In this chapter, we have discussed some of the reasons why sex is not uppermost in women's minds today and why food and eating have become the number one obsession. With the changing roles of women, career demands have become more consuming, and the logistics of fitting sex and romance in to an already busy schedule have created complications. In addition, the current man shortage, the problems of commitment, and the fears of contracting venereal diseases have made sex more trouble than it is worth.

Chapter 7

The Flight from Feeling
and the Lack of Intimacy

> With its title, *Ms.* reminded us in every issue that we were not
> to define ourselves by relationships with men, just as *Self*
> informed us we had an alternative...
>
> —Megan Marshall discussing the Myth of
> Independence in *The Cost of Loving*

In the last chapter, we discussed the situational reasons for women's
declining interest in sex. This chapter is the flip side of the coin and
discusses the internal, more profound reasons for this phenomenon:
women's fear of intimacy. This fear has resulted in an emotional
detachment from sex. Lack of intimacy and feeling characterize many
of the sexual relationships of the 1980s and 1990s. Alice has been
married and has had long-term relationships, but she remains detached
from her emotions during sex. She can achieve the momentary
pleasurable sensations of orgasm, but she has never been able to
"forget" herself during lovemaking. She feels uninvolved, as though
she is observing herself going through the motions. She is unable
to lose herself in the sexual encounter because her self-consciousness
is so pervasive.

Anxieties and preoccupation characterize the sexual relationships of many women. Paula's self-consciousness took the form of
obsession with bodily perfection. Although Paula had a beautiful
body which her husband adored, she was very aware of her stomach,
which she imagined to be protruding and fat. She refused to let her
husband touch her there, depriving herself of pleasure. Her preoccupation with her imperfection took away from her ability to fully
merge with another person. Her anxieties and fears limited her
capacity for intimacy within the safety of a stable, loving and com-
mitted relationship. These self-conscious feelings are so much more

pronounced in a noncommitted, tenuous relationship where one person is scrutinizing the other.

Dee's sexual relationships are also characterized by a lack of intimacy. Dee, a tall, brown-haired, tanned nurse in her early thirties, became sexually active after high school. "You can't believe how sexually promiscuous we were," she revealed. "I screwed and screwed and screwed. That was the thing to do. I don't even remember the number of men I went to bed with, and some men I don't even recall. One time I was at a party, and a man came over to say hello. I asked him if we had met before, and it seems I had gone to bed with him!"

When she was asked what sex was like for her now, she described her latest sexual encounter. "I met him playing racquetball, and we just joked and flirted. I'm really good with that. He took my phone number and we went out later that week and had a great time over dinner. Then we came back to my house, and I asked him in. I always ask them in. In fact, I almost always initiate sex."

When asked why she generally did that, she replied that she liked the warmth and cuddling associated with sex. Then she thought a little longer and added, "I feel like we have to do *something* after the evening is over. This is something I can do...what would I say to him all evening long? We'd really have to get close, and he would get to know me. I am so self-conscious about that. I would not know what to say."

"Do you mean that if you were to talk to him, you might have to get intimate but that if you have sex with him, it could still remain impersonal?" she was asked.

Dee laughed as she realized how strange that sounded. "I guess that's what I'm saying. Sex is an activity that I can do well. It's just the thing to do after a date."

Has sex become so casual and commonplace that it has lost its meaning as an expression of intimacy?

Sherry's sexual relationships are not quite as casual as Dee's, but she too has difficulty experiencing an intimate sexual connection with a man. Although she has been living with Bill for a year, Sherry very carefully points out that she does not want a traditional relationship. She gets enraged whenever he asks her where she is going or makes demands on her time. Sherry makes sure that they each pay their fair share and that both have equal responsibilities at home. Since Sherry teaches a course on the psychology of women, she is very sensitive to male-female power struggles and gets very upset if men whistle at her or view her as a sex object. She does not wear any make-up and lives most of her life in Levis. Sherry seldom shows any vulnerability because she is afraid that this may be seen as female dependency and passivity. Moreover, she can never truly let herself go sexually and is not clear about the reason why.

Sherry's lack of intimacy may have its origin in a fear of merging with another person, and losing her independence in the process. Many women now in their thirties were greatly influenced by the feminist revolution, which warned against dependency on a man and extolled the virtues of career and independence. Megan Marshall, in her book *The Cost of Loving* (1984), describes these women as the Control Generation who were fed the Myth of Independence:

> Month after month, our new way of life was celebrated in magazines designed especially to meet the needs of a new market: ourselves. In their pages the Myth of Independence was solidified into a code by which we could live our daily lives. *Working Women* and *Savvy* told us where to shop for the right navy blue suit, when to trade in a pocketbook for a briefcase, and how to tell a lover you won't leave your job to follow him to another city. *Cosmopolitan* taught us which men to pick up in singles bars, and how to have an orgasm on a one-night stand. With its title, *Ms.* reminded us in every issue that we were not to define ourselves by relationships with men, just as *Self* informed us we had an alternative.... As we agonized over options, gloried in successes and suffered setbacks, we always told ourselves that men could wait. Families could wait. For a long time we didn't even feel lonely.

The fear of merging with another person is very real for women. A passionate sexual experience in which a woman abandons herself can produce feelings of vulnerability and dependency. These can be very frightening to someone who thinks of herself as independent.

JoAnne described this experience: "I was divorced for five years, and I had sex with numerous men—long-term relationships, short-term relationships, doctors, lawyers, Indian chiefs. You name it. I had it. When I met Sean, there was an intense sexual attraction and a very strong chemistry. After we had known each other for just about two weeks, I had this sexual experience which I must describe as unique. It was different not in the technique or foreplay, but in terms of my own psychological response to the experience. It was like I completely lost myself, and I had an overwhelming feeling that I wanted to have a child with this man. I noticed that I did not want to get out of bed, to leave his side, or to do any of the activities or sports I usually love to do. I found myself thinking that all I want to do is be next to this man, to take care of him, to feed him, and to always be near him. On the one hand, this was wonderful. But on the other hand, it was frightening to feel so dependent on a man, to find myself doing things I would not ordinarily do for fear of losing him."

The fear of losing oneself in a relationship may lead to a fear of intimacy, which Megan Marshall terms the new epidemic. Whereas it was once exclusively a male problem, fear of intimacy has now become a female problem as well. As she writes:

> Now women have borrowed it from men, along with the business suits and briefcases. And while the new female fears resemble those of men trying to establish an adult identity, in women fear of intimacy is both more severe and more prolonged. (p. 42)

Megan Marshall adds that while men instinctively know that fear of intimacy will pass, many women adopt it as a way of life. For these women, the major decision of their lives has turned out to be not which career to pursue but whether to give up some of their new-found self-love to love others.

The lack of intimacy inherent in many of today's relationships is in sharp contrast to the overwhelming feelings of passion that characterized love and romance in the 1950s. As more women have marched down career paths, they have incorporated many of the attitudes and behaviors of men. They value their independence and find it difficult to bond with another person. They are afraid of their dependency needs, of becoming vulnerable in a love relationship. In this age, it is easy to turn to something impersonal, nondemanding and seemingly free from conflict—something like food, the new lover.

Food as a lover is always there. It accepts them unconditionally. They do not have to pencil it into their appointment books or worry that it will give them herpes or AIDS. But just as a lover can bring them satisfaction and unhappiness simultaneously, so, too, can food bring emotional upheaval—the dilemma we have mentioned: to eat or not to eat, to be thin and happy or fat and sad.

Chapter 8

When Eating Was Okay

Remember when we used to go to the drive-in and order a hamburger, French fries, and a milkshake and *enjoy* them?

— Woman reminiscing about
the good old days

The conflict—to eat or not to eat—was nonexistent in the 1950s. Eating disorders were rare, and bulimia was almost unheard of. Women did not strain and torture themselves to achieve the perfect body. The consumption of a chocolate bar did not strike terror in the heart of a young, single woman. Women did not think twice about eating hamburgers, french fries, and milk shakes on a Saturday night date. A banana split was a real treat and was enjoyed without inordinate guilt or self-punishment by starvation afterward. Women went out for pizza without keeping track of how much they were eating, how many calories were in each slice, and how long they would have to wait till the next time they could indulge in this luxury. They did not go home afterward and swear to themselves that they would never go out of control again, nor did they race to the bathroom to purge themselves.

Women did not spend most of their free moments daydreaming about forbidden foods. When they fantasized about next Saturday night's date, it was not images of chocolate eclairs that filled their thoughts but images of forbidden kisses. They did not count the number of calories that crossed their lips at each meal. Instead they ruminated about the degree of sexual pleasure they would permit themselves. They did not keep track of the carbohydrates in the baked potato—they kept track of how far they had gone on the previous date and how far below the waist they would permit their partner's hand to travel next time. They did not fear indulging in sumptuous desserts—what they feared was going "all the way." It was as acceptable to eat a chocolate sundae as a stalk of celery. Putting cream and sugar in one's coffee did not create feelings of anguish. Similarly, women did not experience the feelings of deprivation that they do today. If they were hungry for something, they opened up the refrigerator without guilt and remorse. They did not spend their days hungry, deprived, and longing for a feeling of fullness and satiation, nor did they starve themselves and experience hunger pangs or inner cravings. They did not ignore their stomach when it growled at them in hunger. Food was not restricted or forbidden, and they were not obsessed about it.

THE WAY TO A MAN'S HEART

The women's magazines of the time depicted food as a natural part of life, with pictures of the Happy Homemaker cooking and feeding her family spread in technicolor throughout the pages. Women wearing aprons, baking brownies for their children, or tuna casseroles for their husbands could be seen smiling as they fulfilled their roles as wives and mothers. They paid little attention to the caloric content of the white sugar and white flour they used on a daily basis, and they firmly believed in the old adage that the way to a man's heart was through his stomach. The April 1958 edition of the *Ladies' Home Journal* had an article about a new cookbook titled *The Well-Fed Bridegroom* (Williams) which featured an appetizing picture with the caption: "Beef Strogonoff: A Hearty Dish to Keep a New Husband Happy."

Food was an integral part of family life, and a good wife and mother spent a great deal of time in the kitchen preparing food to make her family happy. In addition, she also baked for coffee klatches, bridge groups, bake sales, and church functions. Pictures of the husband, wife, and children sitting together at mealtimes reflected the role of eating as a communal experience and part of the traditional way of life. As one caption described it, "There's nothing like a good meal to keep the family going!"

Since the wife's role required feeding her family three times a day and spending much of the time in the kitchen, food did not have any mysterious or magical value. In fact, in her attempts to stretch the dollar, she often cooked rather uninteresting dishes served family-style. She seldom had occasion to set the table for a romantic dinner for two with wine, flowers, and gourmet delights. Food was not romanticized or sexualized, and nowhere would she come across recipes for a ''sexy soufflé'' or a ''sensually rich chocolate cake.'' Food was so commonplace that it did not have any of the romantic, mysterious, and forbidden connotations that it does today.

She ate openly and without fear, and she did not have to hide in order to eat. The role of wife and mother did not require her to be a size eight. If she put on a few pounds, she was not fearful that she would lose her husband. Society did not expect her—or any other woman, for that matter—to look like a beanpole.

THE NAME OF THE GAME: A PERFECT SIZE TWELVE

This is not to say that women did not worry about getting fat: *they were just not obsessed with it.* A survey of women's magazines of the 1940s and 1950s uncovered very few articles on dieting or weight control programs. There are even fewer on exercising and maintaining a cellulite-free body, in sharp contrast to contemporary magazines which always feature at least one diet plan and several pages of perfect bodies exercising to rid themselves of any ounce of fat.

Although no woman wanted to be fat, her definition of normal weight was very different from what it is today. In one of the few diet articles appearing in the *Ladies' Home Journal* (Norman, July 1955), a woman who lost 100 pounds is seen as now being slim, her dress size only 14 or 16, and her weight 150 pounds. While a 150-pound woman wearing a size 14 or 16 would not be considered slim today, twelve was considered the perfect dress size.

The ideal figure for women in the 1950s can best be described as voluptuous. The huge-bosomed figure, exemplified by Jane Russell or Jayne Mansfield, was the one to which women aspired. These ''mammary goddesses'' (Banner, 1983, p. 283) were the feminine ideal, and the most important film representative of the 1950s voluptuous woman was Marilyn Monroe. Full-rounded breasts, ample hips, and soft, fleshy curves were in sharp contrast to today's muscular, angular bony bodies. By today's standards, Marilyn Monroe, the "love goddess," would be considered too fat, but in her heyday, she was the epitome of womanhood.

Women of the 1950s were more concerned about the size of their breasts than the size of their dress. Having a 36B bra size was just as important then as weighing 110 pounds is today. Women all across the country padded their bras to imitate Lana Turner, the "sweater girl," and at that time no one would have sought breast reduction surgery. Breasts were symbolic of motherhood and the whole nurturant aspect of womanhood characteristic of that era. Big breasts were the ideal of what was considered the ultimate expression of femininity. A flat-chested woman felt ashamed of her body and not like a "real woman."

So while women were not concerned about being ultra-thin, there was a desirable body type and it was just as hard to attain. As there is now, there was a norm then dictating what women should look like. Thin or buxom, the shape of a woman's body has always been governed by some ideal that becomes the norm. A woman who did not meet those norms — be it a 36-inch bust or a weight of 110 pounds — felt inadequate and ashamed.

The rules of the game may have changed, but the game itself remains the same: women have always defined themselves in terms of an external ideal, in order to be acceptable and to be seen as "real women." The external standard of femininity simply reflects the norms of the times. The ideal woman of the 1950s was both voluptuous and motherly, a perfect reflection of her primary roles as wife and mother. Today's perfect woman is thin and sinewy, a mirror image of her role as career woman. Women have always been judged on the basis of their physical appearance. Our bodies are a reflection of how we are evaluated by men, of marriage marketability. We have to conform to current standards of bodily perfection to gain male approval—or do we?

We apparently think so or we would not be going to extremes to conform to a physical standard that is both unnatural and virtually impossible to attain. We would not be risking our health and happiness for an unrealistic cultural ideal. For it is not the size of our breasts or the fat on our thighs that is the issue: underlying the obsession with the body beautiful is the fear that if we do not "shape up," we risk loss of male approval and may ultimately end up alone. And being alone and unloved is the most basic fear women have.

The need for bonding and love is an integral part of the psychological make-up of women. Our ability to nurture and form deep relationships is one of our strengths; it enables us to nurture children and bond families. To be cut off from relational ties because we cannot "shape up" would be tantamount to emotional suicide. And ah, there is the rub: in this era, many of us feel we must almost commit physical suicide to meet our emotional needs.

FROM MAMMARY GODDESSES TO SVELTE SUPERWOMEN

The rigid definition of what constituted the ideal body started to change with the rebellious climate of the 1960s. This decade was characterized as much by a continuation of the traditional values of the previous decade as by an attempt to overturn those values. The new youth culture, with its rock music, sexual experimentation, and pot smoking, started setting new trends in the definition of femininity. Women discarded their cosmetics for the natural look, throwing away their curlers and hairsprays. They stopped spending hours teasing their hair and sculpting it with tons of hairspray into the artificial bouffant style of the time. Instead, they let it grow long and straight. The natural look spread to the body as well, as women discarded the padding in their bras or stopped wearing bras altogether.

The women's movement had a profound effect on standards of beauty for women's bodies. What was considered the ideal feminine body began to change as women changed the definition of their roles. The movement demanded equality betwen men and woman, and a more androgynous body image began to emerge. Unisex clothing came into vogue, and women moved from frilly petticoats to more tailored pant suits. As they rejected their definitions of womanhood, they also rejected some of the body symbols tied to the old roles. The emphasis on rounded curves and voluptuous, milk-producing breasts gave way to a more slender, boyish look. Today's preoc-

cupation with emaciated thinness can be said to have had its roots
in the 1960s.

As women exchanged motherhood for careers and marched in large
numbers into the work force, they exchanged their soft, rounded,
motherly figures for the lean, hard, competitive look. As a woman
liberated herself from her mothering role, she also liberated herself
from her big breasts. The successful woman was slim and angular,
wearing a tailored business suit. Thinness became part of her uniform
and was equated with self-discipline, competency, efficiency: success
in a man's world. To be taken seriously, the working woman could
not afford to present a motherly image.

The lean image conforms to the American work ethic which
admires hard work and self-denial. Slimness symbolizes economic
success, while fleshy bodies represent lack of self-control. To prove
themselves competent and effective, women must look lean and
self-disciplined. They seem to be trying, perhaps somewhat uncon-
sciously, to literally emulate men.

Slimness represented emancipation from the reproductive role, as
Rita Freedman so eloquently discusses in her book *Beauty Bound*
(1984):

> The female body represents fertility and mortality. The flapper
> or the Twiggy look strips it of its fleshy, fruitful dimensions,
> and hides woman's reproductive power behind a neutered
> image. When fashioned as a boyish imp, or most recently
> as an angular jock, the fearful mother figure is deflated and
> safely disguised.

For a woman to be a team player in the business world, she had
to disguise any traces of her reproductive role. As she moved from
the home to the office, she changed her physical body to adapt to
her new environment. Not only has she shaken off the maternal
image, she has also shaken off some of the weak, clinging connotations attached to the female role.

By the 1970s, millions of women had entered the working world.
Not only did they become team members in the office, they aspired
to physical prowess as well. They joined health spas and lifted weights
to develop the lean, athletic, male look. Women replaced the soft,

rounded figure with a well-toned, sinewy body as a new standard of physical beauty started to develop, which included fitness, hardness and tightness. This trend continued and reached excessive proportions in the 1980s, with the new physical ideal described by *Time* magazine in August 1982 as "taut, toned and coming on strong" (Carliss). The cover featured a woman in a leotard.

The new ideal is the embodiment of today's Superwoman, a woman who is equally at ease in the office and the bedroom. She is both competent and sexy, smart and beautiful. She is successful like a man and pretty like a woman, and her thin body reflects both beauty and achievement. Her slimness reflects hard work, self-disciplipne, and symbolizes her accomplishment. Through her perfect body, she announces that she can have it all: look like a woman and succeed like a man. Thinness is the outward manifestation of perfection. Being thin means that she is both desirable and accomplished.

A taut, toned body is the denunciation of the round and matronly figure associated with motherhood. Today's Superwoman does not want to be identified with the happy homemaker who spends her time taking care of her husband and children: she fears excess flesh as a sign of weakness, one that will make her lose not only her status as a peer in the man's world, but also her desirability. For underneath the preoccupation with slimness and the pursuit of the perfect body lies the most basic need for all women—the need to be loved.

This marked shift in the prototype of the ideal female body is nowhere better reflected than in a study of Playboy centerfold models (Garner, Garfinkel, Schwartz & Thompson, 1980), who have grown slimmer every year since the magazine's first publication. Between 1954 and 1978, the average Miss America contestant grew one inch taller and five pounds thinner, reflecting the current obsession with slimness and dieting.

In the past 30 years, we have witnessed a unique phenomenon: food, which was once a natural part of everyday living, has become bad and forbidden, and sex, which was once mysterious and forbidden, has now become commonplace. As we have reviewed the social changes in women's lives over the past three decades, this phenomenon becomes more understandable.

Chapter 9

Consuming Passions

> The guilt that had once attached itself in its most extreme form to masturbation now rested at the bland door of carbohydrates, most particularly upon chocolate and the richer desserts.
>
> —Judith Rossner, *August*

A few weeks ago, we overheard this conversation at the beauty shop. An amply endowed, plump woman was asked by her friend, "Did you spend the weekend with your boyfriend?"

"No," replied the plump woman, "I didn't get any [sex] the whole weekend." She smiled suggestively, "You know what I did instead? I went to See's Candy Store and got the best chocolate I could find!"

Like the woman in the beauty shop, many women substitute oral gratification for their sexual needs. Ellen's addiction to chocolate chip cookies began when she was fifteen, following a heavy "making out" session, which she abruptly interrupted so as not to go all the way. "I raced into the house, opened the cupboard and started cramming chocolate chip cookies as fast as I could." Now, whenever Ellen gets horny, she reaches for the cookie jar.

Jenny, who always watched what she ate and took pains to look slim and presentable, started ballooning after she learned that her husband was having an affair. The first time he was out all night, she went into the kitchen and ate everything in sight. Every night, after her husband would go to sleep without touching her, she would become ravenous and would go on a wild eating binge. For Jenny, food is replacing the sex she does not get from her husband.

Yes, food and sex are related, as illustrated by these vignettes. They are related in how they function and satisfy human needs, and over the last thirty years, the relationship is even more pronounced. We have discussed the magnitude of women's obsessions with food and sex, respectively, and the switch in these obsessions: whereas women use to be obsessed about sex, they now are preoccupied with thoughts and fantasies about food. The focus has shifted from genital to oral gratification, the emphasis from one bodily function to another. Although it may initially seem preposterous that today's preoccupation with eating would replace yesterday's preoccupation with sex, this is not as farfetched as it sounds.

Eating and copulation are two of the most basic human functions. Both are necessary for the existence of human beings and perpetuation of the species. Men and women have organs through which they satisfy these basic urges, and these activities are generally done within a social context. Eating behavior and sexual behavior are primary ways of initiating and maintaining human relationships. In all cultures, people share meals with family or friends, just as they engage in sexual relations with loved ones.

Eating and sex are so closely connected that the same words have been applied to both. People can be hungry or starved for sex, craving it much as they do chocolate. Peter Farb and George Armelagos, in their book *Consuming Passions: The Anthropology of Eating* (1980), cite numerous examples of eating vocabulary used to describe sexual relations and organs. A woman can be referred to as a dish or a hot tomato, and her breasts are also called grapefruits or fried eggs. When a woman loses her virginity, she loses her cherry. Testicles are nuts, while the penis is also a wiener or a banana. To the Aborigines of central Australia the question *"Utna ilkukabaka?"* means either "Have you eaten?" or "Have you had sexual intercourse?" The Sinhalese of Sri Lanka use the word *kanava* to refer to either eating or sexual intercourse. As Farb and Armelagos state: "The close connection between eating and sex is not hard to explain, if it is assumed that early in the evolution of the human species males and females were brought together primarily by the two basic necessities for survival: food and procreation."

Sigmund Freud, the founder of psychoanalysis, developed a theory of human behavior in which he analyzed the connections between eating and sexuality. He believed that people could substitute one type of pleasure for another: they could substitute oral pleasure for genital pleasure. Freud and his followers believed that at each stage of development, different body organs were the primary sources of pleasure. He termed the pleasures derived from eating and other functions sexual or libidinal. Libido was the sexual energy that could move from one bodily opening to another. Hence, the notion of transferring an obsession from one bodily orifice to another is not so farfetched as it may seem.

COMPULSIVE CRAVINGS

The connection between food and sex is so strong that the most successful sex manual of the last decade, *The Joy of Sex* (Comfort, 1972), shares its title with a cookbook, *The Joy of Cooking* (Rombauer & Becker, 1975). The desire to eat and the desire for sex are filled with craving, longing—a yearning to be fulfilled. There is a driven, urgent quality to these passions, an intense excitement. The urgency and passion associated with hunger is well expressed by Kim Chernin (1981) in her book *The Obsession: Reflections on the Tyranny of Slenderness:*

> I look furtively around me, hoping this strong feeling has not been observed. And then I am eating. My hand is reaching out. *And the movement,* even in the first moments, *seems driven and compulsive.* I am not hungry. I had pushed away my plate moments before. *But my hand is reaching* and I know that I am reaching for something that has been lost. I hope for much from the food that is on the table before me but suddenly it seems to be that *nothing will ever still this hunger*—an *immense implacable craving* that I do not remember having felt before. (p. 5) (Italics, ours)

Compare this passage to the following, from Kathleen Woodiwiss' novel *The Wolf and the Dove* (1974):

> The building fires that ran like molten lead through her veins and throbbed with pulsating agony in the depth of her belly only made her seek more heartily his appeasement. That same *intense yearning* began to sweep her as it had only a few hours ago when her young body had responded early to his almost

with a will of its own, meeting his with each deep thrust. Yet when he had moved away she had still ached for his caresses and known *a strange hungering frustration she could not explain.* (p. 181) (Italics, ours)

The desire to eat and the desire for sex share that compulsive, driven quality, the body moving as though of its own will. The drives for both reach their peak during adolescence. As boys and girls enter their teens, their appetites increase, and they can literally eat you out of house and home. Their bodies demand food, just as their hormones surge, demanding sexual gratification. There is a double standard, however, when it comes to freely satisfying these hungers. Whereas boys are actively encouraged to indulge in order to become strong men, girls learn to repress their appetites: both the genital and oral. To get married, a young girl learns that she has to remain slim and to carefully spoon out her sexual behaviors. Thus she suppresses, or tries to suppress, both these natural drives.

The desire for food and the desire for sex are motivated by strong physical urges, which are very highly influenced by thoughts, feelings, and perceptions. For example, we may feel hungry by smelling the aroma of fresh bread being baked even though we have just eaten. Similarly, a pornographic film can arouse sexual feelings even in a sexually satiated individual. Certain emotional states such as anxiety or grief can eliminate hunger completely. Sexual feelings can be extinguished entirely if one is stressed or severely depressed.

Our sexual desire is also influenced by certain sensory qualities like odor and taste. The body aroma of one's sexual partner can be highly arousing as can the taste of body juices. Some men get turned on performing oral sex as their olfactory senses and taste buds get stimulated.

In her book, *Night Thoughts: Reflections of a Sex Therapist,* Dr. Avodah Offit (1981) describes the physical and psychological properties in the food and sex drives:

> The act of eating, then, consists of desire with salivation, the excitement of tasting and chewing, and the orgasmic contractions of swallowing, repeated again and again. No physical act we perform is so like sexual union. (p. 166)

Offit also compares the second part of the eating sequence, the fullness phase, to the sexual response. Feeling satiated is like having a large penis inside, although some people cannot experience this feeling of fullness. Many people cannot tell when they are stuffed with food, just as many are anesthetized to their sexual sensation. Some women eat and eat, but they can never fill their emptiness.

GETTING IN THE MOOD

We use our senses, our thoughts, and our fantasies to enhance both the oral and sexual appetites. The food commercials on television are a good example of how the visual properties of a particular food can cause our mouth to water and propel our bodies to the refrigerator. Similarly, an erotic love scene on the screen can cause the penis to become erect and the vagina to lubricate. We continuously use fantasy to titillate the palate and the pudendum. The Garden of Heavenly Delights could well be a cookbook or a sexy novel.

We all know that there are certain things that can get us in the mood—for food or for sex—and we go out of our way to create an ambience conducive to eating or to making love. Restaurateurs know that and deliberately create an atmosphere that stimulates the appetite. A dimly lit room with soft music, flowers, and candlelight, set off by china, crystal tableware, and artistically folded cloth napkins create a setting where one can dine at leisure and savor the eating experience. An aperitif before dinner, delicate appetizers, a fine wine, as well as sorbet to cleanse the palate between courses, all serve to heighten the taste buds and maximize the pleasure of elegant dining. The beautiful presentation of food stimulates the senses and enhances the desire for it. The rich aromas of delicacies prepared at the table excite the diner, and the anticipation mounts as each ingredient is added. Particularly exciting are those dishes that are flambéd tableside. The glow of the fire coupled with the rich aroma of brandy or cognac ignite the imagination of things to come.

Getting in the mood for sex has similar rituals. We prepare our bodies to be savored much the way the chef carefully prepares a gourmet dish. A great deal of time is given to this preparation, as the body is bathed, moisturized, and perfumed to make it as appetizing and desirable as possible. It is soaked in a hot luxurious bubble bath to make it soft and tender. It becomes amorous as it absorbs the delicious scents of the bath, just as meat soaks in its marinade to absorb the flavors as they mix with the body juices to make it succulent and tender. Excess body hair is shaved, nails are manicured, hair is shampooed, conditioned, gelled, moussed, blow-dried, set, hairsprayed, and carefully brushed and combed into place. Then come the garnishes, in a variety of colors and textures, to create an appetizing appearance. Bright red lipstick, green eyeshadow beneath darkly mascaraed lashes, show off the face to full advantage and make the presentation of its owner appealing, just as parsley and pimento are decorative touches to enhance the appearance of food.

We prepare our minds just as we prepare our bodies to enjoy a dining or a sexual experience. Frequently, these experiences are preceded by feelings of anticipation, replete with thoughts and fantasies. These can occur several hours before the anticipated event and can be fleeting throughout the day. The imagination goes into high gear with the presentation of the menu. As one looks at the numerous possibilities of entrees, together with their descriptions, the mind is flooded with images of the different delights. The appetite gets stimulated by these images, and sometimes making a decision can be sweet agony. As one fantasizes about the different tastes and textures, the desire heightens and the hunger increases. Soon the desire becomes focused on the entree that promises the greatest satisfaction. The hunger becomes more and more intense as one is teased by waiters parading past the table, uncovering dishes with promises of things to come. The arrival of the hard, crusty French bread and the easily spread butter, serves as oral foreplay. The mouth lubricates with heightened desire and the eyes search out the waiter who will bring the long-awaited satisfaction.

We fantasize about an anticipated sexual experience much as we do about an orgasmic food experience. We can have fleeting thoughts of the lover during the day as we go about our business. Pictures of the lover's body, different erotic positions, or types of touches, occupy our mind and fuel our fantasy life. These fantasies become more intense as we come in contact with our lover. Each touch, each gaze, each kiss only serves as a promise of things to come and increases the yearning for consummation. Moist, lingering kisses and the meeting of tongues serve as appetizers for the main course. We start to lubricate as the excitement mounts. Sometimes the foreplay is prolonged and extended, much like a leisurely five course dinner; at other times, it can be as quick as driving through Jack-in-the-Box.

Sometimes anticipation of the main course is not all bliss but carries with it a certain amount of trepidation. Women worry about how much they can enjoy sensual delights and about how much they should eat. Thoughts of the number of calories coexist with images of the delectable dishes. Women learn to curb their desires for calorie-rich sauces so that the fat will not go directly onto their hips. Before they order from a menu, they decide in advance how much they are going to permit themselves. They worry about unleashing their hunger just as their mothers worried about unleashing their sexual desires.

Then, as now, women have had to curtail their appetites and monitor their behavior, for the consequences of indulgence could be disastrous and lead to isolation and loneliness. The irony is that for us to meet our emotional needs, we have had to suppress our physical ones. We have been caught in an ongoing struggle between taking care of our instinctual drives and simultaneously conforming to society's standards of lovability.

The need for bonding and attachment is just as important as the need for food and sex: which one, if any, of these needs should we give up?

THE DOUBLE STANDARD

It is not considered ladylike for a woman to eat large portions of food; however, men are expected to have hearty appetites. If a woman does eat the same amount as her mate, she will unfortunately suffer the consequences of weight gain much faster than he will. In general, men can indulge themselves in greater quantities of food than women and not gain weight. If a man wants to *lose* weight, all he has to do is to reduce his caloric intake to that of the average healthy woman. There is also a double standard for body size between men and women. It is more socially acceptable to be a "big, strapping" man than a fat woman. A man's self-esteem is not as dependent on his being slim. The social and personal rejection of being fat does not extend so dramatically to men.

Similarly, women are not supposed to indulge their sexual hungers to the same extent as men. While men are encouraged to satisfy their sexual needs and enjoy a variety of experiences, women learn to repress and curb those desires. In addition, the consequences of acting out these impulses are more severe and long-lasting for women than men. If a woman transgresses, she is the one who either becomes pregnant, has to undergo an abortion, or simply must carry the label of "loose." The mental and physical effects of her sexuality can stay with her for years and erode her self-esteem. For the good girls of yesterday and today, the consequences of going against society's norms are the shame and ostracism, respectively, of being an unwed mother or having an obese body.

THE "FOOD" RESPONSE CYCLE

In spite of the negative consequences of repressing one's sexual and oral hungers, these drives still press for satisfaction. The appetites demand fulfillment, and the body is propelled into the act of eating or the act of intercourse. Both acts are characterized by a number of phases or stages. Masters and Johnson (1966) list the four components of the sexual response cycle: the excitement phase, the plateau phase, the orgasmic phase and the resolution phase. The eating response is also characterized by stages, leading to satiation: desire with salivation, the excitement of tasting, and the repeated orgasmic contraction of swallowing.

If there is any doubt about the similarities between the sexual and eating acts, compare the following passages, one describing an eating binge, the other a sexual encounter.

> ...Hunger was a distinct pain now. Her mouth began tingling as she thought of the sensation of cold chocolate. She could imagine biting down into the small, hard pieces of chocolate chip.... Mouthful after mouthful. No stopping, not even to sit down. Marge stands at the kitchen counter tasting the cold,

rich chocolate, the sweet whipped cream melting into it. Just this once, she tells herself. Something to make her feel better now. The hungry emptiness in her stomach is disappearing, but the tingling sensation is still on her tongue. (Roth, 1982)

This love scene from Erica Jong's *Parachutes and Kisses* (1984) bears resemblance to the previous passage in the intensity of the desire and the all-consuming nature of the act:

> ...Isadora could feel Kevin's erection against her...and she could feel herself quickening—her cunt moistening, her heart racing.... Kevin fondled her until they both became so excited that they could hardly restrain themselves. He entered her and began to move gently inside her. She felt a sensation she had not known...And as her cunt warmed to him and her spirit warmed as well, she began to come....

In a latter encounter, the similarity between the acts is more striking:

> ...They began to fuck slowly and gently with a kind of rocking motion that echoed through the waterbed. It was such sweet fucking—lacking in violence, but not in passion. "You're yummy," Isadora said, holding him.

Yes, Isadora, sex is yummy, just as food is sexy!

The culmination of a fine meal or an erotic experience is characterized by a feeling of sensual satisfaction and satiation. As Offit states, the fullness phase of eating has obvious sexual implications, in that feeling surfeited may resemble having had an orgasm (p. 167). In eating, there is not one specific point in time during the meal which can be identified as an orgasmic experience. Eating a fine meal can be like having a series of multiple orgasms, each bite offering its own wonderful sensations. When the orgasms are over, there is a content, warm, almost euphoric sensation which can result in feelings of sleepiness, drowsiness, or bliss. Hunger is sated.

Unfortunately, this state of affairs does not always occur: we have all known the disappointment of a lousy meal or a rotten lover. Not all meals are five star—sometimes there is only time for a "quickie"

or junk food—and even those that *are* excellent are not always enjoyed to the fullest. At times, outside distractions, such as a business
call during dinner, can result in a loss of appetite or even indiges-
tion, just as a knock on the bedroom door can result in a loss of
erection. Coitus Interruptus, or interrupted intercourse, according
to Freud, can lead to sexual disorders or anxiety neurosis. During
Freud's time, coitus interruptus was practiced as a form of birth control, with the result that many couples could not enjoy sex.

Sometimes, one not only feels disappointed in a meal but finds
it downright repugnant. This is particularly true with the introduction
of new and strange foods. For some people, steak tartare topped with
a raw egg is enough to make them recoil in disgust. For others, the
delicate tentacles of squid immersed in black bean sauce can produce
nausea. Still others, no matter how hard they try, cannot free themselves from the inhibitions that prevent them from eating raw fish
or letting the slimy oyster touch their tongue. Having to break one's
inhibitions and try these new foods for the first time is akin to breaking
one's initial inhibitions to new sexual activities.

Erica Jong (1984) gives a good description of this initial repugnance
in recounting one of Isadora's lovers attempting oral sex:

> The poor rabbi was a perfect example of this. He went down on
> Isadora as if he were sampling a veritable thousand-year-old
> egg at a banquet on the Great Wall of China, attended, perhaps
> by Henry Kissinger. He went down in a spastic panic as if he
> were about to enter a world devoid of oxygen; you wanted to
> proffer a scuba-diving suit and oxygen tanks—that was how
> panicky he seemed. Eyes closed in dread, tongue stuck out in
> a point (as if hoping to avoid hair), he took the plunge, licked
> a little (thirty seconds' worth, by some imaginary stopwatch),
> and nastily came up for air, and asking, "Was that enough?"

EXCESSES OF THE FLESH

Guilt can change the pleasures of the flesh into a source of conflict. For centuries, society has warned women against the excesses
of the flesh. Nice girls stayed in line and did not let themselves go

out of control. Women learned early to repress their appetite, that is, to keep their legs or mouths closed, depending upon the decade in which they reached maturity. Indulging those appetites, however pleasurable, resulted in overwhelming guilt. Judith Rossner describes this phenomenon in her book *August* (1983):

> The guilt that had once attached itself in its most extreme form to masturbation now rested at the bland door of the carbohydrates, most particularly upon chocolate and the richer desserts. Where once it was feared that the indulgent would suffer from the withering and dropping off of vital organs, swelling and protrusions were now the betraying symptoms of the greedy. Oh, yes, and something called cellulite, which always sounded as though it had been isolated during cancer research. (p. 278)

When women have experienced sexual and oral hungers, it has usually been with the sense of profound uneasiness, a feeling that they could not afford to let themselves get out of control. We have had to learn to put mind over matter, in the never-ending struggle between the spirit and the flesh. We have alternated between being good girls and bad girls, between abstinence and indulgence, fasting and feasting, deprivation and fulfillment.

No matter how hard we have tried to be good girls, the desires of the flesh have been stronger than our will to control them. And every time the flesh won out, we have felt guilty and remorseful. In her book, *The Obsession: Reflections on the Tyranny of Slimness*, Kim Chernin (1981) portrays this condition very well when she describes her indomitable hunger:

> My hunger filled me with despair. It would always return, no matter how often I resolved to control it. Although I fasted for days, or went on a juice diet, or ate only vegetables, always, at the end of this fast, my hunger was back. I had these same feelings about masturbating when I was a little girl. Then, too, it seemed to me that a powerful force would rise up from my body and overcome my moral scruples and all my resistance. I would give in to it with a sense of voluptuous release, followed by a terrible shame. Today, I begin to see that there is a parallel

here. A woman obsessed with losing weight is also caught up in a terrible struggle against her sensual nature. She is trying to change and transform her body, she is attempting to govern, control, limit and sometimes even destroy her appetite. (p. 9-10)

Chernin is no different from millions of U.S. women. The most common New Year's resolution in America is to lose weight, according to a recent study. Unfortunately, it is also the one that is the least successful. People resolving to lose weight lost only one pound— after fifteen weeks! The hunger of the flesh consistently wins out.

Chernin recognizes that this is a lost battle, and in extreme cases, when the flesh wins over completely, the excesses of gluttony and promiscuity rear their ugly heads. These behaviors are considered aberrant, perverse, and sinful in the Christian world. There is a moral condemnation for people who let themselves become so out of control so that they become stigmatized and labeled as sinners.

CONTROLLING THE APPETITES

Toni, an emaciated woman with a long history of eating disorders, described her upbringing. "I come from a very rigid religious background. You would just not believe how strict my parents were. I felt guilty all the time. I learned that I must never enjoy anything. We always wore drab colors, went to church and atoned for our sins. You are not going to believe this, but eating food for enjoyment was a sin. It wasn't just that I was going to get fat, but eating something that tasted good and had calories was like going straight to hell. Binging for me is the sin of gluttony." For Toni, who deprived her body of the "sensual" pleasures, "gluttony" consisted of letting herself eat her fill of hard-boiled eggs.

The sins of gluttony and promiscuity can be washed away by the purification rituals of abstinence and fasting which cleanse the soul and rid the body of its demonic passions. Celibacy is practiced by the most holy of men, and every major religion has certain days during which its adherents abstain from food and sex. Fasting is a purging of the demons and a cleansing of the soul. Fasting and dieting make one feel pure, chaste, and cleansed.

Rudolph M. Bell elaborates on this in his book *Holy Anorexia* (1985) wherein he describes how starvation can lead to sanctity. In the Middle Ages, women with anorexic symptoms were sometimes venerated as saints. Whether anorexia is considered holy or a nervous disorder depends on the culture and the time in history. A holy anorexic, such as St. Catherine of Siena, aimed at spiritual health through self-denial. She died at age 33 in her efforts to subdue her sinful flesh. Unfortunately, she was not unique. Of the 42 women in Italy who were recognized as saints in the 14th century, half exhibited anorexic behavior, according to Bell. All of them saw their body as impure and unclean and fasted in an attempt to cleanse themselves of their bodily sins.

Women have turned not only to religion to cure themselves of their excesses but to the high priests of science, those who practice medicine. There appears to be a clear parallel between the Victorian medical view of women's sexuality and today's attitude about women's bodies. Today, a slim body is a sign of moral character. It indicates hard work, discipline, and abstinence. When a woman steps on the scale, she gets a reading of her moral fiber.

In the nineteenth century, at the height of sexual repression, several moralists developed certain foods to serve as antiaphrodisiacs. "The diet that cured sex" is associated with Sylvester Graham and John Harvey Kellogg. They espoused the degeneracy theory of sex which stated that too much sex, particularly masturbation, was bad for the body and would result in degenerative diseases. To guard against the sin of self-pollution, Graham advocated a regimen of diet and exercise. The recommended diet was a mixture made of coarsely-ground wheat or rye meal combined with molasses or sugar. These ingredients were later formed into plain, thin wafers and became known as none other than Graham crackers, the original antisex diet.

Kellogg's Corn Flakes were originally created by John Harvey Kellogg as a health food, an alternative to wheat. However, this cereal soon became an antimasturbation food and extinguisher of sexual desire, since it was then believed that wheat was a stimulant with aphrodisiac properties. Ironically, John Harvey's brother Keith contaminated the flakes with refined sugar. As John Money states in *The Destroying Angel* (1985): "Just as surely as if their name had been changed from corn flakes to porn flakes, they had lost their virtue as the diet of chastity, abstinence, and sexual purity'' (p. 26).

No wonder our mothers gave us milk and Graham crackers before shipping us off to bed! How come we did not suspect all this time that these innocent crackers would quiet our stirrings? We also did not suspect that when Mom fed us Kellogg's Corn Flakes the next morning for breakfast, it was to reinforce the last night's quietings of our passions. Isn't it strange, now when we look back, that Mom insisted on a good breakfast when we reached adolescence and might harbor erotic thoughts? We marvel at the heights to which society has gone to curb women's appetites!

Peter Gay (1984) describes the late 19th century view of masturbation as both sinful and health-threatening, as well as the remedies to cure women of this dangerous practice. Masturbation, then commonly known as self-abuse, was feared as an epidemic, and a campaign was launched to stamp it out by both the clergy and the medical profession. Self-abuse, or self-pollution, was believed to be responsible for a number of evils ranging from warts, constipation, convulsions, epilepsy, paralysis, and memory loss to insanity or death. A renowned physician of the time declared ''self-abuse'' to be the most certain road to the grave.

Excessive sexual desire which manifested itself in masturbation was considered a disease, and remedies for this disease were provided by the medical profession. These remedies ranged from hot douches to clitoridectomies, and included apparatuses such as chastity belts and a kind of truss that would hold the legs together to prevent insertion of the finger. In reading the literature of the Victorian era, one is reminded of contemporary literature which warns about the dangers of overeating. Read any article or diet book written by a physician, and the message is clear: overeating leads to dire physical consequences—high blood pressure, heart attacks, diabetes, and eventual death. There is an exaggeration to the dangers of excess poundage, just as there was an exaggerated quality to the physicians' warnings and the fire-and-brimstone sermons on the dangers of excessive sexuality. The remedies for these bodily excesses ranged from abstinence and exercise to—when all else failed—surgery.

Remedies for the Sins of Self-Abuse and Overeating

Self-Abuse Through Food	Self-Abuse Through Sex
stomach stapling	cauterization
intestinal bypass surgery	clitoridectomy
abdominoplasty	infibulation (stitching of labia together to prevent masturbation)
surgical suction of fat	surgical suction of sexual fluid
jaw wiring	chastity belts and trusses
steam baths and cold plunge	hot douches and cold baths
body wrap	straitjacket
medication	medication
stringent exercise	stringent exercise
diet	diet

Is there any doubt that today we worry about eating and weight the way our predecessors worried about the expression of female sexuality?

SEXUAL ANOREXIA

The obsession with controlling the excesses of the flesh has resulted in a variety of sexual and eating disorders in women. Anorexia nervosa and bulimia, the diseases of the 1980s and 1990s, are the extreme manifestations of the preoccupation with weight. Anorexia is the ultimate form of self-control. Bulimia alternates between indulgence and denial, doing and undoing, sin and repentance, eating and purging. Judith Rossner (1983) terms these disorders "The twentieth century's abortion on demand for a large number of women to whom sex (or abortion) was no more optional than three meals a day had once been, but whose time between fucking was dominated by anxiety over what they'd last eaten, fear about which craving would next overtake them, and concern over how they would avoid gaining weight when they had (inevitably) binged..."

The anorexic woman is the classic example of using willpower to conquer and subdue the body's urgings. The body and its demands are continuously subjugated; desires are expunged through exercise and rigorous dieting. Anorexia is the ultimate self-denial, a serious illness which can result in death.

As one of the leading eating disorders, anorexia has been compared to a leading sexual disorder, inhibited sexual desire (ISD), the most common and pervasive of all sexual dysfunctions, and one of the toughest to cure. Inhibited sexual desire has even been termed "sexual anorexia" (Hardman & Gardner, 1986). A woman with inhibited sexual desire or sexual anorexia has no sexual desire and derives no pleasure from touching, caressing, kissing, or other sexual activity. Both anorexia and ISD are disorders of the appetite. They are both seen primarily in women; over 90 percent of people suffering from these disorders are female. These women are "starving themselves in the midst of plenty, whether sexually or nutritionally" (Hardman & Gardner). They have turned themselves off from sex or food.

The issue of *control* predominates in these illnesses. The sexual anorexic is afraid to "give in" to her sexuality and blocks out her erotic feelings. The woman with anorexia nervosa controls her body by not eating and by denying her natural appetite for food. Both fear losing control and giving in to their impulses. Just as the sexual anorexic fears becoming promiscuous if she loses control, the anorexic fears that if she eats normally, she will become obese overnight. In both disorders, women deny their primitive bodily hungers and try to rise above them. They starve themselves.

The bulimic woman also starves herself—but not for long. Her periods of starvation are interspersed with periods of excessive overeating. She consumes thousands of forbidden calories, and when she experiences the horror of what she has done, she cleanses herself in any way she can, such as by vomiting or overusing laxatives. Her eating orgies are like a series of one-night stands, filled with disgust and repulsion afterward and a determination not to let this happen again. She repents, over and over, but no matter what she does, she has no control over her cravings, and she gives in to them, time after time, only to begin the cycle anew. Just as the promiscuous woman wakes up with dread the morning after, so too does the bulimic face the morning with remorse and guilt. For her, the "morning after pill" is a laxative.

IT'S DANGEROUS TO TAMPER WITH NORMAL APPETITES

Both the desire for sex and the craving for food are natural biological drives, the natural expression of which has been thwarted by societal rules. As a result, women are driven into abnormal expression of these appetites, with disastrous consequences. The horror of having your jaws wired or your stomach stapled to curb the appetite is no less than the nightmare of having your clitoris removed. The constant guilt, fear, and preoccupation with food and calories is no different from the guilt surrounding sexual behaviors. Anorexia and bulimia are the consequences of the obsessive control of physical drives, just as frigidity, anorgasmia (the inability to have an orgasm), and vaginismus (the contraction of the vagina to avoid penetration) are the results of controlling the natural expression of the normal sexual urges.

Eating and sex are the most basic and primitive of needs. They are life-sustaining, and when they are thwarted or denied, terrible consequences can result. When people are deprived of basic needs, they can go crazy. A person deprived of sleep becomes irritable, and if the situation persists, will hallucinate. A person whose freedom is taken away can become psychotic. People who are chained or locked in closets can go crazy. The need to eat and to release sexual tensions is just as fundamental as the need for sleep or for freedom. Not only are these drives basic on a biological level, they are, in addition, basic on a social level. Human beings are social animals and need human contact for survival. People can literally die if they are abandoned or isolated. When infants are deprived of human touch, they wither away and die. Breastfeeding is the ultimate experience in nurturance. Sharing a meal or a bed with someone is the most intimate form of social contact. Food is love, and sex is love. We need these to survive, and when we deny ourselves these basic life-sustaining needs, we are denying ourselves some of life's most deeply felt experiences.

Women want these experiences. Women want this human contact. Above all women want love and intimacy. Yet they have consistently been forced by society to repress those natural avenues to intimacy. They have denied and thwarted their normal drives, and ironically, in their efforts to be thin or virginal, have sabotaged themselves. At different times in history, they have denied themselves the very basic drives that would provide them with the love and intimacy they crave.

Why are we sabotaging ourselves?

Chapter 10

Food, Sex, Love and Power

Can you imagine a world without men? No crime. And lots of happy, fat women.

—Nicole Hollander, Feminist Cartoonist

The struggle to meet their needs and become their own person while at the same time finding someone to love them has always faced women. If I am truly myself, will he still love me? If I take care of my "selfish" needs, will he stay with me? Historically, women have sublimated their needs, putting the wants, needs, and demands of men first. Women's financial and emotional dependence on men has been so strong that they could not afford to risk losing their main source of support. Even in today's liberated atmosphere, when women are not economically dependent on men, the fear of abandonment still exists. The need for belonging and attachment is so powerful that we are willing to put our health and our bodies through all types of contortions rather than risk being alone. The need for connectedness is so strong that it can overcome the need for self-expression and fulfillment of basic drives.

Why is this universal conflict for women—between dependence and self-expression—manifesting itself through food today? Why have women shifted their focus from sexual to oral obsessions? Why do they turn to food rather than to sex for comfort? What part does the culture play in this world of inhibited sexual desire and increased eating disorders?

FOOD IS MY LOVER

The link between food and love begins at birth. It is mother's milk that physically and emotionally sustains the infant. Food means love, comfort, and fullness; warmth, security, and fulfillment of needs. Food and Mother are interchangeable to the infant. The baby associates food with the warmth and softness of Mother and merges with her in the feeding process. For the infant, food is nourishment at all levels.

As the baby gets older, the strong association continues between being fed and being loved as the mother continues to nourish the child. Cookies and milk can comfort, and chicken soup is a magic potion to make the child feel better. It is not just food, but the act of feeding, that remains wedded to the feeling of warmth and connectedness.

Children learn at a very early age that food helps ease tension. When they are sad and Mother lovingly offers a special treat, the sadness magically disappears. Soon they learn that if they become anxious, they can quell this feeling by a trip to the refrigerator. Food becomes a way to soothe oneself, a way to give one a feeling of peace and security, and besides—it tastes good! Many children who have learned to use food to meet their emotional needs frequently have difficulty distinguishing between true signs of hunger and other feelings. Interpreting any uncomfortable feelings as hunger, they use food to assuage those unpleasant sensations.

That food is used to compensate for lack of love or uncomfortable feelings was poignantly illustrated in diaries that our clients have kept of their binges:

What I Ate	Thoughts and Feelings Prior to Eating
10 Pancakes	I feel so gross. I am so fat and ugly. Here I am, all by
a dozen doughnuts	myself. I am 29 years old and I'm not married and I
half a gallon of ice cream	don't have anyone to love me. I hate myself. I'm all alone.
a bag of Cheetos	

6 Ritz crackers	How am I going to cope? I feel so alone. We are so
4 graham crackers	isolated – not part of anything. No system.
1 quart of ice cream with chocolate sauce	

chicken	I need pleasure, something to fill the void, not feel.
potatoes	
brownies	
cookies	
ice cream with hot fudge sauce	

For many women, food literally fills a void, an emptiness that has no name. When we first met Josie, we could not help but be struck by her overpowering size: Josie was at least six feet tall and weighed in the vicinity of 300 pounds. She was wearing a loud purple and red outfit which only exaggerated her stature. Josie wore her weight proudly, standing tall and straight and looking you in the eye. People who encountered her were intimidated by her, but few knew that underneath her strong exterior was a very vulnerable little girl, a little girl who cried each night and who soothed herself with enormous quantities of food before she could fall asleep. Josie was the youngest child of a mother who adored and overprotected her, a young child who was given lots of love and affection and who worshipped her mother as much as her mother worshipped her. Raised in a cocoon of love, she felt that her mother's affection would protect her forever.

When Josie was eighteen, her security disappeared with the unexpected death of her mother. She was completely unprepared for this loss and went through a long period of lack of control, looking for love. She tried to get love from whomever would give it to her, and these frequently included married men. Most of the time, however, she filled the terrible void with food. She ate and cried herself to sleep every night, but nothing could ever make up for the loneliness and emptiness. For Josie, food was an inadequate substitute for love.

Like Josie, millions of women are trying to feed their empty hearts, to fill the vacuum in their lives with food. Frequently, people turn to food when they lose a loved one. Food reduces the tension and anxiety of being alone; it makes one forget temporarily that one is isolated; it compensates for loss of love. Randi always eats when she is lonesome. She eats when she is sad; she eats when she feels neglected by her lover; she eats when she wants a friend; she eats when she wants comfort; she eats when she is sick.

In Randi's family, food was the magic answer to life's problems. Randi's grandmother frequently fed her bread and butter and oatmeal at night as she listened to her and talked to her. Randi soon learned to equate those foods with love, and as an adult, she would gorge herself with bread and butter while waiting for her lover to come home at night. Randi's lover, a cold, noncommunicative individual, usually reached for the newspaper instead of for her in the evenings, and she reached for the oatmeal bowl. As an adult, she reached for the same foods that soothed and comforted her as a child. Whenever Randi experiences a loss, it is this childhood food that quiets her. Her oatmeal is her grandmother talking to her and telling her that everything will be all right. Food is love, and love is food.

Aggie, too, turned to food when she felt unloved. Aggie was raised in a large extended family that valued the traditions of togetherness. She was never alone, because in addition to her own immediate family of seven siblings, there were always uncles, aunts, and grandparents around. Family gatherings and family reunions were part of her everyday life, and it never occurred to her until she met Charles that she would leave this loving atmosphere. Charles, however, was an attorney with a thriving practice in another state, and it was virtually impossible for him to relocate. It was very hard for Aggie to leave her family and friends when she married Charles, and she could not adjust to life in the new city. She made no friends, as her emotional ties were still with her hometown. Feeling isolated and alone, particularly since her husband worked long hours, she longed to have a child to fill this void, but she was unable to conceive. Aggie became more and more depressed with each passing day, and the more despondent she became, the more she ate.

The only thing she looked forward to each day became her meals. Every morning, she would wait for her husband to leave the house, and then she would watch soap operas and eat and eat and eat until she became sick. The only time she left the house was to go to the supermarket for food. While she ate, Aggie forgot that she was homesick, forgot that her husband left her alone, forgot that she was a stranger in a new city, forgot that she had no baby, forgot that she had no friends. She was immersed with the process of filling up the emptiness inside her. She could never get enough— her hunger could not be quelled.

Clara's hunger could not be quelled either. Clara is a single nurse in her mid-thirties who longs for a husband and family. Her longing becomes more intense with each passing day, and she fears that she will be too old to have children. Her life as she sees it is dreary. She does not like her job but does not have the energy or confidence to look for another one. She has few friends and can count on her fingers the number of dates she has had in the past year. She is lonely and frightened that she will never find anyone to love her. Every night she goes home to her empty apartment, where there is no one to greet her and no one to listen to her. More than anything else, she wants someone's arms around her. She related that when one day at work, one of the doctors, a big, strong, affectionate man, gave her a hug, she literally burst into tears, as nobody had touched her for so long. She was deprived and longed for the warmth of a body next to hers. Sometimes the yearning was so strong, she could feel an ache within her body, an intolerable emptiness.

And so she stuffs herself with food to diminish the ache. Food is her friend and lover, her soother and comforter. Clara eats large quantities of food every evening when the loneliness is unbearable. The more love she wants, the more she feeds herself. Her appetite knows no bounds. "It's strange," Clara said, "but when I'm in love, I am not hungry. When I'm in love, I may even forget to eat."

Marge, like Clara, does not eat when she is in love. When she is not in a relationship she has difficulty controlling her strong passion for food, and she has attended both Weight Watchers and Overeaters Anonymous to help curb her appetite. Marge has been married for thirty-five years to a very critical, abusive, unloving, and sexually impotent man. Marge's eating problem began with the onset of her husband's impotency. Marge enjoyed sex, and it was a very important part of her life. She hungered for sexual intimacy, but her husband would not go for sexual counseling. She soothed her sexual desires by feeding herself peanuts, chocolate, and potato chips. The desire to eat was especially strong at night after her husband went to bed, and she remained alone with her hunger and passion.

The nightly binges gave Marge temporary relief, but she only felt worse the next morning. Because of her religious upbringing, divorce was out of the question. However, she temporarily found a way out of her sexual dilemma. She met a married man and engaged in a long-term affair with him. For the fifteen years that the affair lasted, Marge's eating problems subsided as she was able to meet her sexual needs directly. However, with the death of her lover, she was sexually unfulfilled again, and the midnight binges began. When Marge came to us for help and we asked her what she was hungry for when she ate, she immediately replied, "Sex."

Food is love and sex and closeness and comfort. It soothes and calms and makes the anxiety of being alone magically disappear. As one of our clients told us, "Food is my lover." And food is a very seductive lover. Unlike other lovers, it is always there when you want it. You do not have to wait for the phone to ring, nor do you have to schedule it into your appointment book. All it takes is a few steps to the refrigerator, or a drive through any fast-food place to get your daily love fix. It is...oh...so...readily available. It is always calling out to you: "Taste me, sample me, enjoy me. You know you can't resist me." Food as a lover is so alluring, especially when it is handsomely packaged and shown off in all its glory. "Go on, one bite won't hurt," it tells you. And what's more, food provides instant gratification. There is nothing like rich chocolate ice cream melting in your mouth to immediately arouse pleasurable feelings and help you forget about everything else.

"I love to sit on the couch and watch television when nobody is home and eat Chinese food right out of the cartons," said Jane. "There is nobody to distract me, nobody to ask me to pass the bread, nobody to take care of or worry about except myself. People sometimes ask me why is it that I don't lose weight. To tell you the truth, eating is the only thing I do that isn't preplanned. I work all day long, and it's the one thing that I do that is not routine. It is the only part of my life where I can have total freedom to do whatever *I* want.''

Food as a lover makes no demands. Food as a lover is very dependable—it will not abandon you, and you can always count on it to soothe and comfort when everyone else leaves you. Parents leave, lovers leave, children leave...you can never really count on anyone. But food is always there, ever-present and readily available.

Food asks nothing from you other than that you enjoy it. You can enjoy it by yourself. You do not need a partner whom you have to satisfy. As Jane put it: "Eating is the one thing that I can do just by myself without having to worry about anyone else. Nobody else needs to be involved.'' Many women, like Jane, find eating to be one area in their lives where they can be selfish and put their needs ahead of others. Most of their days are usually spent attending to the demands of other people. After neglecting themselves all day long, they finally have an outlet where they can nourish themselves and let go.

Unfortunately, food is a destructive lover, a double-edged sword. At the same time that it offers immediate gratification and comfort, it insidiously builds up a layer of fat that society states is guaranteed to make one unlovable. Although the cases we have described are extreme examples, the irony for most women is that to be loved, they have to deprive themselves of food which is the most primitive form of love. For a woman to meet her basic dependency needs, she has to deny herself an even more basic need: the need to feed and nourish herself in a reasonable manner.

SEX AND LOVE

Just as food is love, sex is love. This may seem obvious, but it nevertheless needs to be stated. Sex is more than a physical act. Sex involves cuddling, touching, closeness, and the merging of two lovers. It satisfies the primitive needs for bodily contact and touching.

For most women, love and sex are inseparable. To become sexual with someone means becoming vulnerable; it means trusting the other person; it means letting go and abandoning oneself. Sex is love; sex is intimacy.

Why are women today running away from sex as a source of comfort? After all, the women's movement gave us permission to become sexual. We were told that it is now okay for us to express our sexuality—not only okay, but our *right!* Why are we not deriving comfort from sexual relations, especially when we have fought so hard to be able to engage in them? Why isn't sex meeting our needs for affiliation and closeness?

We have pointed out the many disappointments and frustrations that sex and relationships have brought for women today, married and single alike. Career demands, fear of sexually transmitted diseases, and lack of faith in the permanence of relationships have all contributed to a disinterest with sex. Women have learned that sexual relationships would not take care of their emotional needs. For many modern women, the costs of loving have been too high. They have learned that they cannot count on lasting relationships, that they cannot trust men, and they can only rely on themselves. Sex has lost its meaning as the ultimate act of intimacy. It is no longer the merging that can satisfy the most human of needs.

Inez, a veterinarian in her early forties, no longer trusts in the permanence of relationships. When she married José, she thought it would last forever. After their divorce, she sealed off a part of herself and now knows that she can never be truly vulnerable again. She has lived for the last three years with a man who has been divorced and also does not allow himself to get too close. Marriage is not discussed because they are both financially independent individuals who can take care of themselves and see no need to get married. Although they have lived together for three years, they do not include each other in their long-range plans. They have both been traumatized in their attempts at establishing permanency and do not let themselves become emotionally dependent on each other. When they make love, it is not an emotional merging. They both crave intimacy and yet fear it.

Many women, like Inez, have become disillusioned with the transience of relationships and have learned not to expect much from their partners. That way they do not leave themselves open to hurt and disappointment. They have learned that they can only trust themselves, and thus, they turn inward for comfort instead of turning to others. This retreating inward for emotional satisfaction has been dubbed the narcissism of the ''me'' generation.

NARCISSISM AND THE QUEST FOR THE PERFECT BODY

Mary Tyler Moore's face appears in technicolor on the huge screen. She looks like she is in the midst of having an orgasm. Her head is arched, her eyes tightly closed as though she is experiencing an intense physical sensation. Her breathing is heavy, the panting resonating in the movie theater. Her expression is a combination of pain and ecstasy, reflecting the intensity of this experience. Only when the camera sweeps over the rest of her body and exposes her leotards does the audience realize that she is not in the throes of an orgasm but in the midst of an aerobics class. The film is *Just Between Friends*, and Mary Tyler Moore is experiencing the agony and ecstasy of physical exercise.

The intense immersion in self, the rapture that can be achieved alone, and the focus on the body beautiful in a room full of mirrors captures the narcissism prevalent in the 1980s. Narcissism is a pre-occupation with self, a concern with how one appears to others, and with living up to an image. Admiration from others is validation, and the closer one gets to the perfect image, the more self-satisfaction is derived. The modern narcissist has no self other than the image carefully cultivated and honed to perfection. The narcissist is an actress, an impersonator of the self. She is so absorbed with herself and her appearance that she does not have the capacity to love others. Because she is so self-centered that she cannot give to others, she is incapable of true intimacy. The narcissistic female is the Barbie doll and her Ken playmate, both perfectly sculpted, plastic imitations of real people. Not every female is as plastic as Barbie, but one cannot grow up in this culture without adopting some elements of narcissism.

Wanda offers a classic example of a narcissistic preoccupation with slimness. Wanda is a tall, stunningly attractive woman in her early thirties who arrived for her first interview wearing a beautifully tailored high-fashion suit. Her blond hair was striking in its color and shine, with not a hair out of place. She looked like she had spent several hours putting on her make-up and was afraid to cry lest it smear her mascara. She was immaculately groomed, and in fact she later stated that she did not want to make an early appointment because of the amount of time it took her to become presentable. Wanda seemed conscious of her appearance at all times, frequently smoothing her hair or checking her nails. Everything she wore was color coordinated, down to her jewelry, accessories, and nail polish. Wanda certainly did not look like the typical mother of two preschoolers that she was.

Her problem was a mixture of anorexia and bulimia. She restricted herself to a 500 calorie diet but at times went out of control and binged, later throwing up. Wanda was obsessed with looking perfect. This obsession extended to all aspects of her appearance, but particularly to her weight. She worked out religiously in a gym and carefully kept track of her measurements. She weighed herself daily and became horrified when she gained a few ounces. Any tummy bulge was a cue that she looked less than perfect.

Wanda made herself the sole focus of her attention. She was certain that every pound she gained would be noticed by others and that people would comment if she gained weight. Her conversation was centered around herself and the image she was trying to present. She was also concerned that her new house be a model of exquisite taste. She wanted her husband's business associates to see her as the model hostess. She wanted her children to look just right because they reflected her image. Wanda was so consumed by her image that that was all she was. She derived her personhood by the reflected admiration she saw in others.

Today's narcissism may be related to some of the broad societal changes. With the high divorce rate and no guarantees of permanent partners and providers, women have learned to turn to themselves for sustenance and satisfaction. They have been encouraged by therapists to "look out for Number One," to be their own best friends, and to seek self-actualization at all costs. Women have been reminded repeatedly not to be self-sacrificing like their mothers. The new cultural ideal is the Superwoman, the woman who can do everything and do it well, the woman who is validated for achievement rather than for providing nurturance. The plump, matronly, middle-aged wife and mother, now pityingly referred to as the "displaced homemaker," has been replaced by the young, slim, competent career woman who achieves financial reward, status, and admiration from men. Women are finding out how much more gratifying it can be to have a career that carries status than to stay home and be "just a housewife."

"LEAN AND MEAN"

The increasing number of women in the work force has reinforced the growing emphasis on self and achievement. At the same time, the long hours and energy required to compete leave little room for relationships. Working women no longer make their husbands and children the center of their lives. The modern working woman has no time to bake cookies or to be den mother. Try as she can to be with her family, she must use some of her time to maintain her professional image. This means shopping for a working wardrobe, keeping abreast of the latest developments in her field, and maintaining a slim silhouette.

The images of successful women are images of youth, beauty, and slimness. The nurturing, mothering images of the past are no longer relevant. Golda Meir and Eleanor Roosevelt would need an image consultant if they wanted to compete in today's world. Successful women in their fifties and sixties can no longer afford to look their age if they want to survive professionally in today's youth-oriented society. Barbara Walters, Joan Rivers, Joan Collins, Elizabeth Taylor, Nancy Reagan, Helen Gurley Brown, Jane Fonda . . . all women over fifty . . . these are the images and role models that flash on the screen for women to emulate. These are all Superwomen—women who have achieved fame and fortune while they look young and beautiful—and *thin*.

Today's women are being told that they can do it all, that it is possible to succeed in the masculine world and remain feminine and desirable at the same time. Consequently, women are trying to be Superwomen, to have it all and to do it all. The Superwoman is equally at ease in the corporate boardroom and between the satiny sheets in the bedroom. Beneath her pinstriped suit she wears a black lace bra. The message is, "Work hard, but don't forget to look good. Be feminine."

Thinness carries a myriad of meanings for women. It represents both beauty and success. It is a sign of a woman's femininity and beauty as well as personal accomplishment. Thinness, thus, becomes a symbol of the modern women's quest for perfection. Through her perfect body, she proclaims that she can do it all: look like a woman and succeed like a man. In trying to live up to this image of perfection, she becomes a victim of the diet and fashion industry. Since both beauty and success are a matter of effort, the inability to attain the perfect body makes a woman a failure. The less than perfect body announces a lack of will power or discipline to achieve this task.

Thinness is also a rejection of the ample, matronly, rounded body of Mother. Being plump and rounded reminds one of the traditional woman, the dowdy, matronly homemaker who spends her time cleaning the house or taking care of children. The espousal of the lean, muscular look is a turning away from the rounded, female stereotype of the prefeminist era. Being curved, rounded, and soft is a sign of laziness, a sign of not taking care of oneself. "Look at her, how she's let herself go," we say, when a woman puts on a few pounds. Excess flesh is a sign of sloppiness, and the Superwoman is afraid that if she lets herself go in that area, she will lose status, power, and control. She will show weakness.

Thinness is a status symbol, just like designer clothes. Thinness is very important to a woman's professional image. It means that she is in step with the times. In many professions, how a woman looks is just as important as her capabilities. A television newscaster can no more afford to gain a few pounds than to forget her lines. Being thin is part of the image of success, and even women who have rebelled against the cultural pressure to remain slim have ultimately succumbed to it. Linda Ellerbee, a successful and competent reporter by all standards, had to go to a spa to rid herself of excess poundage to contribute to her television show's success. Being thin means that you are competent and disciplined; you are staying in shape—physically and otherwise.

Women in executive positions with large companies are particularly vulnerable to the pressure to look slim. They represent the corporate image, and they need to represent it well. How they look is a direct reflection of their company's image. Recently, a friend in New York told us this story: "I had lunch with a business acquaintance whom I have known for years. I hadn't seen her for about six months, and she had lost a lot of weight since our last meeting. I commented on how good she looked, and she said to me that she was told in no uncertain terms by the powers that be that she would have to lose weight if she wanted to go anywhere within the company. She said, "In order to work for _____ Company, you have to be LEAN AND MEAN!"

"Lean and mean" is an old term in the corporate world, referring to the qualities of successful male executives. This phrase has become the buzz word for women today in the business environment, as they are forced to imitate male behavior on the road to success. Being thin is not a luxury for the majority of career women who want to be successful. "Lean and mean" suggests success, toughness, strength, and competence. It is a statement that a woman is living up to the professional image of someone in control of her destiny. The slim woman serves as a role model for others, and she cannot afford to let them down.

Being thin is also a sign of beauty and desirability. Beauty has always been important to women, and a woman's physical attractiveness was in direct proportion to her success with men. The social opportunities for women are more affected by their physical beauty that the opportunities for men. Although ideals of beauty have changed over the years, the importance of physical appearance has not changed. There is very little doubt that the eating disorders we see today are a direct result of society's increasing idealization of slimness as the model for female beauty.

One would think that women who do not depend on men's approval would be free from the obsession with thinness. That does not seem to be the case. Lesbians, too, have internalized the cultural standards of bodily perfection and have incorporated slimness as a value. Like most other women, lesbians are concerned with the amount of fat on their bodies. They want to look fit and athletic and struggle with internal demands to conform to society's standards. The struggle may not be as intense as for heterosexual women, as suggested by this story. Evelyn, a friend of ours, described her feelings about her body before and after coming out. "When I was with a man, I thought a lot more about what my body looked like," she said. "I worried if my breasts were too small or if my hips were too big. When I was straight, I struggled a lot more with this issue. I still struggle with it but not the way I did before."

To be thin is to be beautiful and lovable; to be fat is to be ugly and undesirable. The moral values inherent in the terms *thin* and *fat* are well expressed in Linda Myer's poem *My Mother's Prayer* (1982):

> No one will love you if you are fat.
> No one will *have* you if you are fat...
> Thin is good.
> Thin is beautiful.
> Thin is right.
> Fat is blight.
> Fat is ugly.
> Fat is lonely.
> Fat is bad.
> Fat is sad.

Research has shown that women who accept the "Superwoman" ideal uncritically, that is, want to be warm, nurturing, and feminine while at the same time succeeding in their careers, are most likely to have eating disorders. Many women search for the perfection symbolized by the perfect body, pursuing slimness as an obsession. Thinness is a combination of the seemingly incompatible goals women set for themselves. Thinness says: Yes, you can have it all—you can look like a woman and achieve like a man. When the scale registers the magic numbers, it tells you that you have made it, that you are now okay and can feel safe that you will be loved. For after all, "No one will love you if you are fat."

WOMEN, WEIGHT AND POWER

Just as thinness carries with it a myriad of meanings, so too does fat. Any phenomenon that exhibits such a nearly universal negative impact on women has to be analyzed from within the cultural context from which it derives. Laura Brown (1985) does an excellent analysis of the issue of power as an element in women's struggles with food and eating. She contends that the paranoia over getting fat exhibited by women can only be understood from within a culture where women are devalued and stripped of power, a culture which has a stake in the increased invisibility and powerlessness of women. In this culture, a woman is only good if she is small and does not occupy space. A "good" girl does not "throw her weight around." She is too threatening if she is seen as having "substance" and can only be valued for being a "little woman." A fat woman is considered ugly and bad because she is visible and takes up space.

Fat women also break the cultural rules against powerfulness in women in that they feed themselves. In a society where women's powers are seen as threatening, a "good" girl does not nurture herself in any direct or straightforward manner. Her role is to nurture others, particularly males, placing their needs above her own. If she should feed herself, she does so in a manner that induces guilt and promotes self-hatred. Thus, when a woman eats, she feels guilty and bad. Rather than enjoy the experience, she feels remorseful about it and does penance for her sins by fasting, dieting, and depriving herself.

Being large and feeding oneself are both ways in which women break the rules against personal power. A woman who feeds herself and does so without guilt is going against this most basic of messages given to women. A fat woman clearly breaks these fundamental rules: she occupies space and feeds herself. Fat is an expression of personal power—that is why it is so feared, hated, and avoided at all costs by so many women.

Fat oppression, the fear and hatred of fat people, remains one of the few "acceptable" prejudices still held by otherwise progressive persons. Being fat is not the problem but being fat-oppressed is (Brown, 1989). Fat-oppressive attitudes and actions are so pervasive in the lives of women that many of us do not even question the dictum that fat is bad, ugly, unhealthy, and to be avoided at all costs. In the next chapters, we explore some ways of dealing with this insidious energy drain.

THE NEED TO BELONG

"What do women want?" Freud and others have asked this question. In a recent cartoon, a woman responds to her husband who has been asking this question: "What do women want? I'll tell you what women want. Women want *men*...that's what women want." This simplified, humorous explanation sums up the psychology of women: women want to be loved and often will do anything for love.

An old poem says that love is a woman's whole existence. This statement is as true today as it was then. In spite of the women's liberation movement and the changing sex roles, women still see the love of a man as the most important priority in their lives. Clara, a successful, attractive editor, expressed a feeling of emptiness and a strong desire to share her life with someone. "I have so much to give," she said, "and nobody to give it to. I know I'm okay. I know I'm good-looking. I have a terrific personality. I feel good about myself...but what is it all worth without someone to share it with?"

"I want to wake up Sunday morning and have brunch with someone. I want someone I can snuggle with under the covers. I want to travel with someone. Life is okay, but I don't feel I am really living until I can find someone to love." Clara's composure slipped and she appeared ready to cry: "I am so tired of always looking for potential partners. That is all I think about. I have good friends, I have a wonderful family, and I can entertain myself, but a very important part of my life is missing. I *need* to belong to someone, to buy presents for him, to do things for him, to share my life with him. Even though I can take care of myself, I *need* to be attached to someone."

The need for attachment and belonging is a core element in the psychology of women. Our dependency needs are an integral part of our emotional make-up. The need for a stable consistent relationship starts at infancy and remains through adulthood. Women have a very strong need to emotionally attach themselves to a partner who will give them nurturing, psychological sustenance, and physical contact. We need the safe haven of someone for love and protection and feel hollow and empty when our needs for bonding are unmet. Like Clara, we may describe ourselves as incompete when we do not have a lover. This desire for connectedness is so strong that it has been theorized as having a biological basis.

Although men have needs for bonding, intimacy, and attachment, these are not significant components of their identities. Women's sense of self, on the other hand, is organized around being able to make and maintain relationships. We define our worth in relation to others more than men do. We measure our self-esteem within the context of relationships and judge ourselves in terms of our ability to care. Carol Gilligan discusses the differences between women and men's needs in her book *In a Different Voice* (1982). The "different voice" expressed by women focuses on the care for others' needs and on the value of connections and attachments between people. Women's caring, intuitive responses are in marked contrast to those of men. Gilligan points out that one voice is not necessarily better than another, just different, and that this difference should be respected and valued. When women deny their affiliation needs and try to become like men, they develop an emptiness that comes from suppressing a very important aspect of their personality. For us to deny our dependency needs is tantamount to emotional death.

Megan Marshall also discusses the importance of women accepting their dependency needs. In her book *The Cost of Loving* (1984), she emphasizes the role of the feminist movement in creating the Myth of Independence. "If a woman was lonely, according to the Myth, it was because she was weak, probably not ready for marriage anyway. Wanting a man was a sign that something was wrong: a modern woman should enjoy solitude." Marshall writes that when women have adopted the Myth of Independence and denied their dependency needs, they have paid a high price emotionally. When women deny a very important aspect of their identity and try to "be like men," the result is emptiness, dissatisfaction, and psychological devastation. She states that women need to recognize that their selfhood runs deeper than simple competence in the business world, that finding someone to care for and who will care for them is an even more important aspect of their core.

Nancy Chodorow also emphasizes the importance of relationships in women's lives. In her book, *The Reproduction of Mothering* (1978), she argues that the qualities of caretaking and nurturing are an integral part of the female psyche, and are inevitable as long as women are biological mothers. She sees women's anatomy as creating a worthy, rather than an unfortunate, destiny. Nurturance and bonding are as much a part of being a female as are breasts and vaginas. A woman can no more disown her psychological identity than she can her physical identity. Just as men and women differ physically, so do they psychologically. Chodorow and Gilligan claim that there is a dual model of human development, one for men and one for women. Men have a basic desire for independence, in contrast to women's drive for "inter-dependence." When women have denied their needs for affiliation and "inter-dependence" by trying to fit into a man's world, they have severed the roots of their identity.

UNHEALTHY DEPENDENCY

It is important to distinguish "inter-dependence" from unhealthy dependency needs which, rather than allowing women to express themselves fully, inhibit them from reaching full adulthood. Penelope Russianoff terms this unhealthy behavior "desperate dependence" in her bestseller, *Why Do I Think I Am Nothing Without a Man?* (1982). Desperate dependence is different from the normal human experience of needing and caring for others. It is the clinging, helpless, childlike behavior exhibited by many women today. There is a desperate quality to the need for a man, and the woman looks to him to save or rescue her. She is frantic without his approval and feels that she cannot survive without his constant validation of her, that she does not have a life without him and that she is drowning in a frightening world without him by her side. When she is around him, she sometimes regresses to the level of a spoiled child, becoming demanding and sometimes self-destructive. In a state of desperate dependence, a woman *loses* her selfhood, often adopting his needs as her own, whereas in a healthy interdependent relationship, she experiences her identity fully.

Unhealthy dependency is also the main topic of Colette Dowling's bestseller *The Cinderella Complex* (1982). As Dowling writes:

> ...*personal, psychological dependence—the deep wish to be taken care of by others—is the chief force holding women down*

today. I call this 'the Cinderella Complex'—a network of largely repressed attitudes and fears that keeps women in a kind of half-light, retreating from the full use of their minds and creativity. Like Cinderella, women today are still waiting for something external to transform their lives.

Unhealthy dependence stifles psychological growth; healthy dependency enhances it. Unhealthy dependency generates feelings of helplessness and powerlessness; healthy dependency creates feelings of confidence and security. Unhealthy dependency produces passivity and a sense of inadequacy; healthy dependency enriches the self. Unhealthy dependency fosters insecurity and a fear of risk-taking; healthy dependency permits creativity and spontaneity. A woman locked in a state of unhealthy dependency feels like a child and needs a parent figure to rescue and protect her, in contrast to the fully functioning adult woman who expresses her dependency needs in a healthy manner.

Desperate dependency in its most extreme form results in masochistic behavior. A woman who feels totally helpless without a partner will tolerate all forms of physical and mental abuse to keep her lover from abandoning her. Robin Norwood's bestseller, *Women Who Love Too Much* (1985), discusses unhealthy dependency as "loving too much," where being in love becomes equated with being in pain. The unhealthy dependency is translated into an addiction which takes a very heavy emotional and physical toll on the woman. The woman who loves too much will endure the pain of infidelity, beatings, name-calling, and all kinds of indignities in order to remain in an unhealthy dependency, sometimes even endangering her life and that of her children. "Loving too much" becomes synonymous with masochism. Some women will do anything for love.

WHAT ARE LITTLE GIRLS MADE OF?

If we investigate the roots of this strong need for affiliation and approval, then eating disorders become more understandable. Somewhere in our development, we were carefully taught that being loved was necessary for our survival.

There are specific expectations of men and women in our culture which are so pervasive that people cannot grow up without integrating them into their personalities. Before the baby is even born, parents visualize a soft, pretty baby girl or a husky, strong baby boy. Although girls are initially stronger than boys, they are perceived as more fragile. They are handled more delicately, and they are rescued from crying more often than are little boys. They learn early on that help comes quickly if they ask for it, and becoming rescued and protected becomes expected.

Girl babies are rewarded for clinging, dependent behavior, being discouraged from exploratory, adventuresome activities. Excessive concern about a baby girl's safety is shown by her parents before she is even able to walk, with fathers engaging in much less rough-and-tumble play with their girls than they do with their boys. Since risk-taking is discouraged in little girls, they learn not to trust themselves and lack confidence.

By the time the child is six, patterns of independence and dependence have developed. Males have experienced numerous situations where they have been encouraged and rewarded for mastering some skills. A boy feels good about himself in terms of what he achieves. When he is left alone with his building blocks, he creates towers by himself and is proud of his independent achievement. He begins to develop a sense of pride and self-esteem that is not so dependent on others' approval. He derives a sense of achievement and mastery from what he can do by himself. He is being rewarded for achievement and independence.

Girls, on the other hand, have been encouraged to be "good" and not to take risks; they are left alone less frequently than boys. A good little girl stays clean, keeps her room tidy, and looks adorable. She is rewarded for playing quietly with her dolls, for not making any noise, and for not being any trouble at all. In fact, approval is gained by not making waves. "She was such a good little girl all day," her mother will brag. The little girl is not rewarded for what she achieves but for how pleasing she is to others: how well she gets along in relationships. Thus, affiliation needs are reinforced and become all-important to women. We get our self-esteem through external validation. Approval from others, rather than mastery for independent tasks, becomes the chief motivating drive. Through our cultural upbringing, we learn that we cannot rely on ourselves and that we need someone to take care of us and approve of our behavior. "Daddy's little girl" is always rescued, the hope being that someday she will get married and have someone to look after her and protect her.

Girls also learn their behaviors of dependency, passivity, and accommodation through observing their mothers. Role modeling is the way we learn appropriate sex-role behavior, and little girls are eager to imitate same-sexed adults. The little girl may observe that Mommy takes care of Daddy and is very much involved in the emotional well-being of the household. Relationships are very important to Mommy, who works hard to please Daddy. Mommy is always soothing, cajoling, comforting, and pleasing.

All of this relates to the development of strong affiliative needs. That means she values relationships above anything else. Since the little girl is brought up under more parental protectiveness, receives less encouragement for independent behavior, and is rewarded for being socially accommodating, she is more apt to distrust herself and to need the protection of a loved one.

"SHE'S SO PRETTY..."

That a woman needs someone to love and protect her is implicit in the fairy tales she hears at bedtime. Snow White, Cinderella, Sleeping Beauty, Rapunzel...all beautiful damsels in distress who wait patiently for their prince to come and rescue them. Love means being happy, being taken care of, and everything turning out happily ever after. There is one big catch, however, to achieving eternal love and happiness: you must be pretty. Nothing other is asked of the princess than to be beautiful. All the princesses attained love for no other reason than that they were beautiful. Homeliness was associated with wickedness, and the stepmothers and witches are always ugly, ending up dying or being left alone.

Beauty and being the right size were emphasized in these ancient tales much as they are now. Cinderella's stepsisters were envious of her small shoe size and tried everything they could to stuff their oversized feet into the glass slipper, just as women today will do almost anything to mold their bodies into a size 6. Cinderella won everlasting love and happiness from the prince because she had the perfect sized foot.

Girls learn the importance of looking pretty at a very early age. As soon as they have a few strands of baby hair, it is fastened with a ribbon. Many girls have their ears pierced before their first birthday and their nails polished by their second or third. Rita Freedman discusses the socialization of women in their attitudes toward beauty in her book *Beauty Bound* (1986). Little girls spend hours putting on their mother's make-up and playing dress-up, learning early in their lives that femininity and beauty are one and the same. Their wardrobe is much larger than that of their brothers, and they are frequently told they look pretty, especially when they wear dresses.

Books for school children also emphasize the importance of looks for girls. Female animals are frequently pictured with ribbons on their tails and long, curly lashes. Fairy tales, of course, both implicitly and explicitly emphasize the importance of being beautiful.

Children's toys also contribute to the importance of prettiness as a feminine value. Boys are give action toys to play with, whereas girls are given dolls with stunning wardrobes. The Barbie doll has been one of the most popular dolls for little girls, and millions of dollars have been spent by parents in outfitting this pretty doll. Toy stores not only sell glamorous doll outfits, many sell doll make-up! Little girls get their own make-up kits, learning very early to imitate Mommy and make themselves beautiful by dabbing color on their faces and painting their fingernails. The little girl is taught the importance of looking good before she is even ready for elementary school.

By the time girls reach high school, looks become the key to popularity and success. High school girls spend a great deal of time looking in the mirror, trying different hairstyles, make-up, and wardrobes to achieve the "perfect" look. Each pimple becomes a catastrophe, and a cold sore will keep her isolated in the bedroom, bemoaning her fate. Each female adolescent is convinced that she is the epitome of ugliness and will never be as pretty as her peers. She never has enough clothes—or the right kind. She spends hours in shopping centers looking at the latest outfits, trying them on endlessly. She learns that the prettiest girls get the most attention from males, and it is their attention that gives her an identity. Thus, she spends hours upon hours perfecting her make-up and wardrobe so that she will be beautiful and worthy of male attention. The number of dates she gets is a measure of her self-worth. Beauty is power, and power is beauty.

As young girls mature, the pressure to be beautiful of face and body persists. So women continue to spend hours in front of the mirror, at shopping centers, and in exercise classes to make themselves objects of male desires. When a woman has a boyfriend, the first thing she is asked is, "What does he do?" When a man has a girlfriend, the first thing he is asked is, "What does she look like?" Beauty is still the most important criterion in defining a woman's appeal to men.

Dustin Hoffman is said to have described as "shattering" his realization that, although he could portray a woman in the film *Tootsie*, he could not be a *beautiful* woman. Being a plain woman was very different from being a plain man. Being ugly can be a disastrous experience for a woman. Being ugly and being unlovable are one and the same. No wonder so many women diet themselves into ill health.

Being beautiful today means more than possessing a pretty face. Slimness is a very strong component of the definition of beauty. Women entering beauty pageants are judged by how they look in a bathing suit, and the standards of bodily perfection reflect slimmer and slimmer bodies. Our obsession with slimness is an overadaptation of the cultural ideal of beauty in vogue today. The focus on beauty as a central feature of a woman's identity has existed since women were looked upon merely as possessions of men, and their market value depended on their appearance. Today's strong emphasis on slimness is a natural extension of this historical phenomenon. Has anything really changed?

STILL TRYING TO BE GOOD GIRLS

In spite of the social progress of the last few decades, women will still do anything for love. We continue to follow society's rules of lovability and do not question standards of what makes one attractive to the opposite sex. We continue to make tremendous sacrifices to be "good" in society's eyes. Being a good girl means conforming to what is accceptable—it means placing one's marketability on looks and doing what is required to please a man.

The good girl constantly watches herself, constantly fears making a mistake. From the time she is a little girl, she learns to "behave," to be a "perfect lady," and not disrupt others, for her love and approval depend on being "good," on being perfect. Whether perfection is a taut hymen, as it was 30 years ago, or taut muscle tone, as it is today, it is always the starting point of the road to love, travelled by wandering women with weary feet and growling stomachs who plod along incessantly, ignoring their bodies' cries for both physical and psychological fulfillment.

Chapter 11

Breaking Free

Inside every emaciated woman lives a healthy woman waiting to be fed.

—Stella Jolles Reichman,
Great Big Beautiful Doll

Can I pig out now?

—Typist, after completing
the last chapter

So, all right, here we are, having read this far in the book, recognizing the good girl in each of us, and understanding the lengths to which we will go to gain love and approval. What do we do now that we recognize our self-defeating behavior? How can we satisfy our need to be loved without denying our natural urges? Can we find love and happiness without going hungry? Is it possible for us to free ourselves from the obsession with dieting and slimness? How can we meet our needs for attachment and acceptance without constantly depriving ourselves of our basic desires? There *are* answers to this seemingly impossible dilemma. We *can* free ourselves from the trap that we have created for ourselves. We *can* rid ourselves from much of the needless worry and daily agonizing. We *can* stop being obsessed about food and return to the natural activity of eating. In this chapter, we offer some specific ways that women can change their actions and break free from their self-defeating behaviors.[1]

---

1. Women with diagnosed eating disorders need to seek professional help.

CHALLENGING THE RULES: WHY SHOULD MY HAPPINESS DEPEND ON A NUMBER ON THE SCALE?

The good girl has always followed the rules. From the time she was an infant, she was loved for being good. Being a good little girl meant that she remained quiet, did not mess up her room, and did whatever Mommy and Daddy told her. She did not question the limits on her behavior that adults set for her. These were the rules, and they had to be followed. The reward was lots of cuddling, kissing, and praise for her compliance. With time, she learned that following the rules was the way to win approval and affection. Challenging the rules could mean loss of love. There were many spoken and unspoken rules of conduct for a young girl. All of these were geared to make her valuable in the marriage market. Conforming to society's rules today means conforming to unrealistic standards of bodily perfection.

Women can challenge and free themselves from the impossible standards of perfection applied to their weight just as their sisters liberated themselves from their sexual shackles. Women can open their eyes to the conflicting messages that society has placed upon them and realize the paradoxes inherent in these messages. The double messages are humorously portrayed in a recent comic strip, in which ''Cathy'' bemoans women's situation:

> They filled the world with workout tapes and then put a chocolate chip cookie stand on every corner.... They cheered us to the peak of our careers and then said we have ten minutes to start having children.... They mellowed us into more realistic goals and then showed us a woman with a 41'' rear get married to a prince.... They said we could have it all, and then charged $200 for boots. Now—overweight, confused, broke and frazzled...

The first step for women is to recognize the absurdity of the irrational demands that they have swallowed hook, line and sinker. Women need to become aware of the craziness inherent in the conflicting messages that bombard their senses daily. They need to wake up and see the ridiculousness of trying to live up to impossible standards of perfection.

Joan, an attractive young woman, was plagued by anxieties and persistent thoughts of inadequacy because her scale did not register the magic number. Never mind that she was well within the normal range of weight for her height and bone structure; never mind that she was big-boned as was every member of her family; never mind that she felt healthy and strong at her current weight. The only thing that mattered was that the scale did not register 110! With therapy, she woke up to the realization that she had been letting society dictate what she should look like and how much she should weigh. "Why should my happiness and self-worth be based on some arbitrary number," she asked, "a number I didn't choose."

As Joan became aware of how she had let society dictate what she should look like, she became very angry. Anger is another step in the process of liberating oneself from the crazy-making double binds. It supplies the energy to promote constructive change. It was only when women recognized the sexual double standard and became angry about it that they made changes that brought them sexual freedom. Anger was the force that helped them liberate themselves from their sexual shackles.

Joan was even angrier when she realized that had she been born thirty years earlier, her buxom figure would have been applauded. What is fashionable in body shape and size changes from decade to decade, and for a woman to remold her body to adapt to the times is not only ridiculous but impossible to achieve. At different times in history, different body types were in vogue. Frail, sickly, and fragile, devoid of muscle tone and pure white skin never touched by the sun—that was the ideal prototype in the early part of the nineteenth century. The rounded woman dominated the late nineteenth century where big busts and big hips were "in." The round, buxom type was also popular in the 1940s and 1950s. The ideal prototype in women's body shapes changes with current fashions, and for a woman to remold her body just as she does her hemline borders on the absurd.

We tell women, "What would you do if Madison Avenue decreed that every woman should wear a size 5 shoe?" "That's ridiculous," they say. "Each of us have different sized feet. We can't change that." Yet in China, women used to do precisely that. Their mothers would bind their feet to make them small and delicate. Absurd, you say? No more absurd than trying to get everyone to fit into a size 5 dress. We need to understand how we have let ourselves be manipulated by the cultural standards of bodily perfection promoted by the media. We need to question these artificial standards just as our sisters challenged the sexual rules dictated to them by society.

EXPLODING THE MYTH: DOES THINNESS BRING ETERNAL LOVE AND HAPPINESS?

When women questioned and changed the rules about their sexual behavior, they found out that this did not result in a loss of love. They got married even though they were not virgins. They learned that being a good girl was not necessarily the road to love and happiness. Women are learning this lesson in the business world today. They had always believed that if they were good girls at work, they would be rewarded. So they worked hard, put in long hours, smiled at their bosses, and did whatever they were told—only to lose the promotion to someone else who did not follow the rules. Many career women, to their chagrin, are finding out that being good does not lead to a pot of gold at the end of the rainbow. Being good does not give you a raise. Following the rules does not always work.

We not only need to challenge the absurdity of the "good girl" rules, we need to ask if following these rules *really* brings the promised rewards. "Will being a good girl sexually really bring me love?" "Will being a good girl at work get me a raise?" "Will being thin really make a difference in my life?" "Is thinness the magic road to happiness?" In our practice, we have women challenge the notion that thinness will automatically change their lives. "What do you think will happen when you are 110 pounds? How will your life be different?" we ask them.

Sometimes we ask our clients to do the following exercise to get them in touch with their unrealistic expectations of what being thin would mean. They are to write down the first thought that comes to their minds as they complete these sentences:

"If I were thin, men would ...."

"If I were thin, I would ...."

"If I were thin, my life would ...."

"If I weighed ten pounds less, I would ...."

"If I looked good in a bikini, I would ...."

Kelly, a strikingly beautiful young woman of normal weight made her lifetime goal the ability to lose ten pounds by the summer so that she would look stunning in a bikini. "What would happen then?" we asked her. "I guess men would look at me." "Don't they already?" "Yes, all the time." "Then, what?" we prodded further. "Suppose *every* man looks at you and finds you attractive? What would happen then?" Kelly smiled sheepishly. Many women, like Kelly, find, to their dismay, that nothing happens when they reach their weight goal. Even women who are not blessed with Kelly's beauty and near perfect figure discover that the world remains essentially the same when they lose weight. As one of our clients put it after she got rid of her fat: "I thought if the fat would go away, I would be happy all the time. Now I am thin, but I still have the same problems." Life is difficult for everyone, whether they weigh 110 pounds or 150 pounds. There is pain whether one is fat or slim: there is pain in just being alive. Thinness will not automatically bring joy; it is not a panacea for happiness.

Women need to detach thinness from any other connotations. The loss of five pounds is only losing five pounds of fat cells, nothing more and nothing less. It is like getting rid of five inches of hair or losing your suntan. You are still the same person underneath. Being thin does not automatically mean being confident. Being thin does not mean being happy. Being thin does not necessarily mean being beautiful or sexy. Being thin does not make you perfect. We need to detach thinness from the myriad of meanings we have assigned to it, just as in the past women detached the multiple connotations they had given to having a simultaneous orgasm. Many women believed that experiencing an orgasm at exactly the same time as their partner would guarantee sexual and marital bliss. If they would only achieve a simultaneous orgasm, they would be complete women and their lives would be perfect. They learned, to their chagrin, that this standard of sexual perfection was no insurance against divorce, depression, or feelings of inadequacy. An orgasm is only an orgasm, and ten pounds are only ten pounds.

EXAMINING THE COSTS: IS IT WORTH DYING FOR?

In addition to challenging the unrealistic standards of perfection currently demanded by society, women need to examine the high price of conforming to these destructive norms. What are the costs of trying to live up to these ideals? We pay a very high emotional, physical, and financial price when we adapt to the current standards of bodily perfection.

In addition to the millions of dollars spent on diets and weight loss programs, the heaviest price that women pay for conforming is the loss of a healthy body. The physical complications associated with excessive dieting include fatigue, malnutrition, menstrual irregularities, anemia, dehydration, electrolyte imbalance, hypoglycemia, headaches, and a high susceptibility to infection. Starvation can lead to the inability to think clearly, lethargy, sleep disturbances, and depression. Excessive exercise as a form of weight control can result in amenorrhea and eventual problems in their ability to have children.

Women who binge and purge experience even more severe medical problems, some associated with the binging and some with the different forms of purging. Kidney failure and heart complications are some of the problems associated with eating disorders. Hypokalemia, a low level of serum potassium, is probably the most serious complication from binging and vomiting. If untreated, it can result in kidney failure and cardiac arrest. Throat blisters and the wearing away of the tooth enamel can result from vomiting. Ironically, although many women engage in destructive eating behavior to look good, this may result in some very unattractive features, such as rotten teeth, loss of hair, or ugly skin eruptions. Using laxatives to control weight can lead to laxative dependence and sometimes irreversible changes in lower-gastrointestinal-tract functioning.

"I never thought it would happen to me," said Janet, after she paid $9,000 in dental bills to repair the damage created by her vomiting. Many women, like Janet, although aware of possible physical consequences from destructive eating behavior, deny that it can happen to them. Surprisingly, even nutritionists who are all too aware of the consequences of malnutrition starve themselves. Too often and to their distress, they realize the physical damage they inflicted on themselves in their pursuit of slimness.

Dieting in its extreme form is starvation which can lead to death. The untimely and shocking death of Karen Carpenter illustrates the very heavy cost of adhering to unrealistic standards of bodily perfection. Fortunately, most women do not go to the extremes that Karen Carpenter did.

However, even constant dieting can result in medical complications. Evelyn has been on a diet for as long as she could remember. In her early teens, she was able, through dieting and strenuous exercise, to go down to a svelte size five. She was very proud of her accomplishment, and received lots of compliments on her good figure. To maintain her slim frame, Evelyn had to fight her body's desire to put on weight by constantly limiting her caloric intake and working out rigorously. She jogged for an hour every morning and went to aerobics classes nightly. Evelyn stopped getting her period three years ago. She considered that only a minor problem until recently when she and her husband were trying to conceive. Evelyn will do anything to have a child—except the one thing her doctors tell her to do: gain weight and limit her exercise. Evelyn did not think it could happen to her.

The pursuit of thinness has emotional consequences as well. Not eating right can by itself result in feelings of tiredness and depression. The feelings of constant deprivation and gnawing hunger can lead to weakness, irritability, and mood swings. Anxiety and lack of concentration also accompany poor eating habits. Rachel could not understand her constant mood swings. She felt on top of the world in the morning, but by afternoon, she was filled with anxiety and could cry at the drop of a hat. She became irritable and could not concentrate on her work. Her typing errors frustrated her even more and added to her edginess. By the time Rachel got home from work, she had a headache and was practically shaking. Was Rachel having a nervous breakdown? No, she was just on a diet!

Megan could not understand why she had so little energy. Most of the time, she felt so tired and lethargic that all she wanted to do was lie on the couch and watch television. Megan could not understand the reasons for her exhaustion. After all, she was in her early twenties, perfectly healthy, and had no unusual stresses. She had a relatively nondemanding job and very few responsibilities after work. She did not appear to be depressed over anything in particular that would account for such fatigue. But, for the past three months, Megan had been on a thousand calorie diet, and her feelings of apathy and depression were related to her lack of sufficient nourishment.

Being on a diet means feeling constantly hungry and deprived. The feeling of deprivation can be so extreme that it becomes a major preoccupation. When the body is hungry, it keeps sending messages to the brain that it wants to be fed. Obsessive thoughts and images of food preoccupy the mind and color the thinking. When these messages are ignored, there is an overwhelming feeling of denial and deprivation. The person on a diet feels constantly frustrated on both a physical and emotional level. "I hate the feeling when I am on a diet," said Ellie. "It restricts me so much from doing anything. I can't go out for lunch or social gatherings because there is food there. I have to walk away from office parties because someone will force a piece of birthday cake on me. It is so frustrating to have to watch everything I eat. I feel so deprived. I want to scream." Feelings of anger and frustration are very unpleasant consequences of constantly watching what you eat.

Social isolation invariably results from an intense focus on remaining slim. Like Ellie, women will avoid social situations which involve eating so that they will not be tempted to eat. They will restrict their socializing to prevent themselves from going out of control in the face of tantalizing food. They evaluate most social events in terms of how they will affect their current diet. Since most social activities include sharing a meal, their activities are limited considerably. These women end up sitting at home alone on Saturday nights and missing out on the very social interaction that they crave.

Social isolation is also a price women pay when they do not feel good about their bodies. Many women are afraid to be seen before they reach their "perfect" weight. Thus, they will avoid going to the beach, the swimming pool, or the tennis court, lest they expose their less than perfect bodies. If they do go to the beach, they will cover their bodies and feel hot and sweaty, rather than wear a bathing suit and enjoy the water. Women miss out on so much *fun* just because they are so self-conscious about their bodies. As one woman said, "I can't wear my bathing suit today because I'm too fat. I'll wear sweat pants." Another one said, "It is so uncomfortable to always hold my stomach in!" Women deprive themselves of so much fun because of their obsession with slimness. They are so preoccupied with how they look that they cannot enjoy the experience. They miss out on friends, on activities, and on life! They cannot enjoy the comraderie and closeness that they most crave because of their intense inward preoccupation. The cost of this self-absorption is too high.

Loss of self-esteem is another price that women pay in their struggle for perfection. Women feel guilty because, regardless of their efforts, they are unable to reach model-thin proportions. They constantly compare themselves to younger and slimmer bodies and feel hopelessly inadequate. They develop feelings of inferiority and cannot accept themselves the way they are. They feel depressed because they cannot measure up to the impossible standards they set for themselves. They feel that there is something desperately wrong with them.

Women begin to hate themselves and their bodies when they do not conform to the cultural standard of slimness. Sometimes the self-hate is so intense that suicide is contemplated. "I can't stand my body! I hate it! It's disgusting!" said Mimi, a woman who had gained ten pounds recently. Mimi disliked her body so much that she could not make herself look in the mirror. She felt that she was the most ugly and loathsome person around, and that she should not even be around people. Her feelings of self-hate colored her thinking about herself to the point that she was constantly crying and could neither sleep nor concentrate on her work. Her depression had reached clinical proportions, and she needed medication to help her function. Depression is a large part of all eating disorders and is a very high price to pay. Is it worth it?

ACCEPTING THE BODY AS IT IS

Women do not need to feel depressed and inadequate because their bodies are not perfect. Instead, we can learn to like and accept our bodies as they are, with all of their imperfections. Is it *really* possible to do that? "You have got to be kidding!" women tell us. "How can I ever learn to live with those thunder thighs, much less like them? I will *never* accept the jiggling cellulite! It's not possible!"

It may seem impossible at first, but lots of women have become friends with their bodies. They have learned to appreciate their bodies and become comfortable with them. They have started to see their bodies as sources of pleasure rather than as objects of pain. How can women begin to accept their bodies? We offer some suggestions that have worked for many women. We suggest the Body Mirror Exercise developed by Lonnie Barbach in her book *For Yourself: The Fulfillment of Female Sexuality* (1975) as a starting point. The exercise involves looking at oneself without any clothes on in a full-length mirror. To get the maximum effect from this experience, women can pretend that they are from another planet and that they are looking at their bodies for the first time. To see the body in a new and different way, a brown paper bag with holes for the eyes can be placed over the head. This gives some women distance and objectivity. They are to look at the body from all angles and positions, either squatting, sitting, or standing. They can alternate between standing very straight and slouching and pushing their stomachs out. If there are any parts of the body that are considered particularly unattractive, such as a protruding stomach or sagging breasts, the woman can exaggerate these imperfections until she starts to become more comfortable with them. For example, she can push her stomach in and out or bounce her breasts in a playful manner. The aim of this exercise is to become comfortable with the body and to learn to appreciate it. As the woman studies her body from all sides and angles, she can note specific aspects of it that she finds pleasing. She can write down those particular parts of her body that she finds attractive. For example, she might become aware of the smoothness of her skin or the shapeliness of her legs. She can learn to appreciate the curve of her body and the way the particular parts blend together.

Many women, when doing this exercise, are surprised to find that there are some attractive aspects to their physical shape that they had not noticed before. For example, women who have focused solely on the width of their hips were pleasantly surprised to note that this made their waist seem small by comparison and created an hourglass silhouette. We ask women to focus on their positive features when they do this exercise instead of narrowing in on the imperfections. We ask them to see their bodies with loving rather than critical eyes.

We tell women to value their body parts for the functions they perform and for the pleasure they provide. A woman can appreciate her breasts, regardless of size and shape, because they can nurse an infant and because they can feel so good when sexually stimulated. She can value her hands for their dexterity and movement. They allow her to touch, to play the piano, to plant flowers, and to perform an endless number of tasks. She can derive so much pleasure from using them to create a sculpture or to feel the smoothness of a baby's soft skin. Women need to use a criterion other than outward appearance for evaluating their bodies. When it comes right down to it, what is most valuable about each body part is that it functions and that it is healthy. If the body is viewed in its totality, we can only marvel at the beauty with which it operates.

Ingrid, who used to be obsessed with her physical imperfections, learned a new-found appreciation for the workings of her body. She expressed the joy that each part of her body gave her. For example, she wrote:

> My hair...I do not particularly like how my hair appears to others. I do not enjoy the style. But for me, and my lover, I love the way it feels: soft and light. The color is rich and shiny. I love how it falls down over my face and I love when my lover enjoys my hair...

> My eyes...the soul of my mind and body. They are incredible instruments. They allow my brain to see the world. I can see such colors...

> My feet...I love my feet. So far from my brain, yet still so connected and vital to my body. The pounding they take, whether walking or supporting me when I run...

Like Ingrid, we can learn to appreciate our bodies for the functions they perform and for the pleasurable feelings they create. In the long run, the most important aspect of the body is that its parts work in harmony and perform their functions. A healthy body is a valuable asset.

We encourage women to make a list of what they value about their bodies and write an affirmative statement for each body part. This may be difficult to do at first. If they have a block about particular body parts, they can use humor to remove those blocks and to become friends with their body. A good illustration of humor used to pay homage to thunder thighs is reflected in a poem brought to us by one of our clients:

These hips are mighty hips.
These hips are magic hips.
I have known them to put a
spell on a man and spin him
like a top!

Women can see some of the humorous functions in their less than perfect body parts. They can see the funny side of having small breasts or protruding stomachs and not take these imperfections so seriously. Women who have difficulty making a list of positive affirmations about their body can write a humorous ode to it.

This is not to suggest that outward appearance is not important or that women should not pay attention to improving their appearance. It is the *excessive* attention given to having a slim body that is neurotic. When a woman spends most of her waking hours being obsessed with her weight and lets her moods go up and down with the scale, then something clearly is wrong. She has let her priorities become lopsided. Women can realize that factors other than weight constitute physical attractiveness, and they might be well advised to spend the time they worry about their weight in making other changes in their appearance. Getting a new hairstyle, wearing different make-up, or experimenting with new colors usually contribute to a more noticeable change in appearance than losing or gaining a few pounds.

Another exercise for enhancing body image, particularly for rounded women, is suggested by Stella Jolles Reichman in her book *Great Big Beautiful Doll* (1977). She tells the big woman to close her eyes and to think of all the round shapes that mean happiness, light and warmth:

> Think of a ball that bounces and elates us, a hoop that spins and twirls, a colorful balloon that rises freely above our cares, a whirlpool that suggests the mystery of the sea, the sun for warmth and light, the moon for mystery and romance, the earth we live on, and the most perfect shape, the egg, the symbol of life.

She then asks them to think of the skinny shapes:

> Sticks, knives, arrows, lightening—all of which suggest destruction. Small are germs, pests, worms, jealousy, and selfishness.

> So put all such thoughts of being skinny behind you. Keep thinking BIG for we are visually as well as spiritually close to heaven, more in tune with the universe, and more at peace with the world. (p.31)

Women can use similar visualization to validate and appreciate their body size. They can learn to see the positives in their roundedness and bigness, even if they are not ''in'' according to the current fashion for body type. For example, a big woman can visualize herself as ''majestic''; a full-breasted woman can start to see herself as ''sensuous'' rather than as ''fat and dumpy.'' Women need to realize that regardless of what they do, there are certain aspects of their body that they cannot change. As a petite blonde woman told us, ''No matter what I do, I can never be a tall, black male.'' Certain aspects of our bodies remain with us. We cannot change our bone structure, our height, or our basic body configuration. We need to accept those unchangeable aspects of our bodies and see them in a positive light.

An exercise that has been helpful to women in learning to accept their bodies involves having a conversation with the body part that is most troublesome. The first step is to lie down, with paper and pencil nearby, closing the eyes and breathing deeply until a state of relaxation is achieved. In this state of relaxation, the woman can concentrate on the body parts that she likes the least and the feelings that these body parts evoke. She is to pay attention to the thoughts that come to her consciousness, for example, "my stomach is ugly, my thighs look sick, my breasts are lopsided," and so on. She can then open her eyes and write down all the words and thoughts that have come to her mind, no matter how silly or irrational they seem. After completing the list, she can talk to those body parts and tell them how she feels about them. She can talk to them in any tone she chooses, using harsh and critical language to tell her body how she feels about it.

Following the lashing out at her body, she can then switch places and take a few minutes to imagine what it is like to be those troublesome body parts. She can put herself in the place of those parts and *become* her breasts, thighs, or stomach. What is her body feeling after being berated so harshly? If her body could talk, what would it say? What feelings would it have about the treatment it has been getting? What would it say about how it has been mistreated? How does it feel to be labelled "sick", "ugly," or "lopsided"? How would they like to be addressed? On a separate page, the woman can write down what she imagines the different body parts think and feel. For example, the thighs can say, "I feel sad and hurt to be seen as sick and ugly. I feel hurt that you always hide me and cover me up. Why do you hate me so much? Why do you put uncomfortable girdles on me until I can't breathe? I have served you well for thirty years. I let you sit on me, I take you hiking all over the country, and you know you can always count on me. I would like you to talk to me in a nicer tone of voice. I want you to put comfortable shorts on me so that I can breathe the fresh air once in a while." The dialogue with the body can be the start of a new relationship with it. Women can begin talking about their bodies in a kinder way and treating them with care and respect. They can start becoming friends with their bodies. These changes, of course, do not take place overnight, but with time, acceptance of the body becomes possible.

Treating the body with care and respect is very important. Treating the body with love means dressing it with beautiful clothes instead of covering it with colorless sacks. It means buying those clothes now rather than waiting till a size six is attained. It means dressing for *now* rather than some elusive future date when bodily perfection is achieved. It means buying bright, contoured styles rather than "fat" clothes. It is only an illusion that one looks less heavy with loose garments than with fitted ones. Putting nice clothes on the body is saying to it that it is worthy of expensive clothes. It is announcing that it is valuable rather than an object of shame to be hidden and camouflaged.

Even if a woman does not like her body, we tell her to begin to behave as though she does and to act as she would if she were a smaller size. In the process of being nice to her body, she can start learning to like and accept it. Behaving as though she likes her body means doing away with "fat postures" just as she does away with "fat clothes." Fat postures include slouching, crossing the arms to cover the body, or standing behind other people to prevent others from getting a good look at the shameful body parts. Women report that when they are feeling thin, they walk, stand, and move in a different manner than when they are feeling fat. We encourage our clients to adopt the open postures that they use when feeling thin even at those times when they feel bloated, heavy, or disgusted with their bodies. Just as we tell them to wear "thin" clothes, we also tell them to adopt "thin" postures *NOW*. We tell our clients that as they start to treat their bodies with love and respect, they will gradually grow to like them.

THINKING HEALTHY INSTEAD OF THIN

Liking the body means taking good care of it by feeding it the proper nutrients so that it can function well. Just as we feed it good thoughts, we also need to feed it good food. Women can repeat to themselves, "Good food, good thoughts." We have already discussed the many health hazards resulting from destructive eating habits. Both starvation and binge-eating can lead to disastrous physical and psychological consequences. Feeding the body properly means eating three meals a day rather than skipping meals and feeling hungry all day long. The feelings of deprivation invariably lead to binging and create a yo-yo syndrome of gaining and losing weight. Women believe that the fastest way to lose weight is through virtual starvation. Unfortunately, when a woman subsists on 500 calories a day for a long period of time, her body adapts to that caloric level, and her metabolism changes. Then, when she increases her caloric intake, she gains weight. It is important, whether a woman wants to maintain her weight or lose a few pounds, that she eat three nutritionally balanced meals a day. Many women fear that they will balloon overnight if they let themselves eat breakfast, lunch, and dinner. However, they find that they do not gain weight if they allow themselves to eat normally. In addition, they do not overeat because they feel neither ravenous nor deprived.

Many women divide food into two categories: "good" food and "bad" food. "Good" food is tuna fish, carrots, celery, and hard-boiled eggs. "Bad" food is pizza, rice, bread, tacos, ice cream, and pie. We tell these women not to view food as either good or bad. Food is food, and they need to permit themselves to eat whatever they want. They may have to limit their portions, but they are not to view any food as off-limits. Viewing a certain food as a "no-no" only makes it more tantalizing and creates an obsession with it. If there is a particular type of food that they absolutely love, such as chocolate chip cookies, they need to make room for that in their daily allowance, just as they make room for certain luxuries in their budget.

Feeding the body properly is important whether one is a compulsive overeater or dieter. We encourage women to think "healthy" rather than to think "thin" when choosing what to eat. "Healthy" means including meats or other sources of proteins in their diets, as well as carbohydrates such as breads, rice, or potatoes. Fruits and vegetables also supply the body with needed nutrients. If a woman is intent on losing weight, we encourage her to cut down on fats and sugars rather than deprive herself of the body-sustaining nutrients. Women can learn to eat wisely, that is, in a healthy manner.

Taking care of the body also includes some form of exercise. This may seem contradictory as we have described at length the excessive emphasis that women have placed on exercise in their attempts to achieve the perfect body. It is the obsessive exercise that is neurotic. When a woman spends two or three hours a day, *every day*, in vigorous aerobic workouts because she feels unloveable otherwise, then she has lost perspective of what is important. When she exercises not to feel healthy as much as to feel worthy, then something has gone wrong. Exercise should not be a form of self-flagellation and a beating of the body to get it into shape. Exercise can be done with love and care for the body, not to make it thin but to make it healthy. Eating and exercising properly *in moderation* is healthy. Excessive eating and exercising are damaging to health. A glowing, healthy body is much more attractive than a sickly, emaciated one.

When women have asked men what they considered sexy or alluring in a woman, men have responded that a woman who looks healthy is most sexy. Interestingly, most of the features that men associated with attractiveness were nonphysical ones, such as a sense of humor, confidence, or a genuine laugh. Appealing "behaviors" are so much more important in defining one's attractiveness to the opposite sex. As Rosalind Russell said, "Living well is a woman's best cosmetic" (*Reader's Digest*, July 1984).

BECOMING PERSONS INSTEAD OF PRODUCTS

Although it is natural for women to want men to find them attractive, they need to question whether in their efforts to look good, they have packaged themselves as products to be evaluated by men. Women have a long history of offering themselves as objects to be auctioned. In the past, they packaged themselves as virgins in order to be acceptable in the marriage market; today, they package themselves as svelte superwomen so that a man will marry them.

As Susie Orbach (1978) puts it:

> She is brought up to marry by "catching" a man with her good looks and pleasing manner. To do this she must look appealing, earthy, sensual, sexual, virginal, innocent, reliable, daring, mysterious, coquettish and thin. In other words, she offers her self-image on the marriage marketplace.... Since women are taught to see themselves from the outside as candidates for men, they become prey to the huge fashion and diet industries that first set up the ideal images and then exhort women to meet them. (pg. 20)

Although many well-educated career women do not like to think of themselves as objects to be evaluated by men, they are surprised to find that in their actions they behave as products on display for the ultimate buyer: the male. We ask women to do the following exercise to help them become aware of their need to behave like products instead of persons. We ask them to take a sheet of paper and put two headings across the top. On the left, they are to put "HOW I BEHAVE WHEN I AM ALONE WITH OTHER WOMEN," and on the right, they are to write "HOW I BEHAVE AROUND MEN WHOM I FIND ATTRACTIVE." Then they take a few minutes to think before listing their responses under the separate headings. Women report that they "perform" more for men than they do for women. They make more of an effort to look good and say the right things. They are more self-conscious around men and try harder to please them. They report behaviors like holding their stomach in when around men, taking more time to apply cosmetics, and trying to be witty, bright, and sexy. With other women, they can relax and be themselves. In other words, they present themselves as products, giving men the power to evaluate them.

Women should stop thinking of themselves as products. Being products suggests powerlessness. We need to realize that we have more to offer in relationships than the physical body, and that we are more than our bodies. As we become aware of our "product-like" behavior, we can start experimenting with small changes. For example, the next time that we catch ourselves worrying, "What will he think if I give my true opinion?" or "Will he still like me if he sees me without my makeup?", we can take a risk and behave as we would with a girlfriend. We may find that it can be a big relief to relax and be ourselves!

Women have discovered that they have a lot to gain when they start thinking of themselves as persons instead of products. When they have used men's approval as mirrors of their self-worth, women have felt insecure because their self-esteem depends on some fluctuating external standard. The excessive need for external approval can lead to an unhealthy dependency on men. Rather than looking for outside validation, we need to trust our own perceptions. Women should learn to be their own judges of their adequacy rather than let other people or the media validate them. Becoming our own person is an ongoing process for many women because our approval from others has always depended on being good girls and following the rules. We need to stop thinking of ourselves as good girls and start thinking of ourselves as adult women. We should stop viewing ourselves as products and start seeing ourselves as persons.

NOURISHING THE SELF

Being their own person does not imply that women should deny their normal needs for affiliation and bonding. We need to accept our needs for closeness and recognize them as legitimate. As we have said before, women's needs for attachment and belonging are a core element in their psychology. Unfortunately, these needs have been equated with powerlessness and the negative aspects of the traditional feminine role. When women deny their healthy dependency needs and try to become like men, they may develop an emptiness that comes from suppressing a very important aspect of their personality. It is then that they turn to food as a lover. Food is convenient, handy, and makes no demands on them. Women can learn to meet their needs for love in constructive ways and to nourish themselves without turning to food.

In her book, *Feeding the Hungry Heart*, Geneen Roth (1982) states that on a physical level food is a nourishment and on an emotional level food is a nourishment. We can learn to meet our needs for nurturance by first taking care of ourselves. Good girls usually do not take care of their own needs. They put other people's needs ahead of their own and frequently end up feeling tired, empty, and drained. It is then that they turn to food to fill up this void. Many women say they feel guilty spending money on themselves and taking time out for their own pleasure. They feel that they are being selfish by trying to meet their needs. The truth is that if we do not take care of ourselves, we will not have the energy to give to others. We will be too tired, irritable, and drained to reach out. In order to be loving to others, we first need to be loving to ourselves. We need to take care of ourselves at a very basic level. That means seven to eight hours of sleep every night, three nutritious meals, and some "alone" time to recharge our batteries so that we can have the stamina to meet the numerous daily demands. This may seem self-evident, yet women frequently deprive themselves of food, sleep and relaxation while tending to the care of others.

Nourishing the self means more than satisfying these minimum requirements. We can learn to nurture ourselves much as we do someone we love. We can draw on their abilities to "mother" by mothering ourselves. We can start thinking of ourselves as someone we love and who needs loving kindness. We need to be aware of the emotionally needy child within ourselves and pamper that child. We can nourish ourselves through our thoughts, our behaviors, and our caring relationships.

Women can, first of all, nourish themselves with good thoughts. "What are some things you say to yourself that make you feel good?" we ask our clients. We ask them to think of what they would tell a lover, friend, or a child they love. For example, they can say to themselves, "You handled that very well," "You look really smashing today" or "Sit down and relax: you deserve a break." We tell our clients to be especially kind to themselves when they have made a mistake. Many women are harsh on themselves and make statements to themselves such as, "You dummy, you blew it again!" or "How could you be so stupid?" or "You look disgusting today!" Many women, when they listen to their self-talk, are surprised at how critical and self-punitive they are. Some say they would not talk to their dog the way they talk to themselves. They need to make a conscious effort to feed themselves nourishing thoughts.

Besides thinking good thoughts, women can nurture themselves in a number of other ways. Listening to music, taking a nap, or reading a magazine from cover to cover are ways of replenishing the self. "How can you give yourself a treat?" we ask our clients. Pampering the body by taking a bubble bath, having a manicure or pedicure, or getting a massage were listed as special treats. Other ways of nourishing the self are trying on new clothes, attractive lingerie, or a sensuous new fragrance. Some women feel they can nourish themselves most by taking time to engage in physical activities that they consider fun, such as dancing, swimming, or taking a walk.

Talking to friends can be particularly nourishing. We can receive a great deal of pleasure from our relationships with others. We ask our clients to think of people in their lives who make them feel particularly good about themselves and what it is that those friends do to make them feel good. For example, we like to be around people who are not critical or judgmental and who accept us the way we are. We tell our clients to develop their nourishing relationships and spend time with people who feed their self-esteem. We need to recognize how important our needs for attachment are because it is through love and intimacy that we get nourished at the deepest level. We need to accept our dependency needs and strive to satisfy them.

DEVELOPING A "HEALTHY SELFISHNESS"

Research has shown that those who are most at risk for developing certain eating disorders are women who strongly espouse the traditional female role. They are other-directed, compliant, and have a very strong need to please others—in short—they are co-dependent. Co-dependency is a popular term which essentially means putting others' needs ahead of one's own and investing a great deal of time and effort in taking care of others instead of oneself. For example, young women may choose careers that would please their parents instead of themselves. Married women often take over most household duties even when holding a full-time job because they see it as part of their feminine role.

It is important to note that compliant, pleasing, subservient patterns of behavior are learned—we are not *born* being people-pleasers. We learn these behaviors by modeling the actions of other significant females around us. Children watch and imitate their elders and get rewarded for being accommodating. The most important sex-role model of a little girl is her mother, and by observing her mother, she learns what is appropriate gender behavior. She also picks up what is appropriate behavior with the opposite sex through her relationship with her father. Often, fathers reward sweetness and compliance in their daughters. Many little girls, by observing their mothers, learn to cater to Daddy and to work hard for his approval. This other-oriented, accommodating behavior is reinforced by Daddy on a daily basis, and it becomes an integral part of the girl's psyche. The little girl's people-pleasing extends to and is reinforced by other people in her life, such as teachers, aunts and uncles, or grandparents. As she grows up, the compliance becomes a part of her personality so that she may not even be aware of how much she has learned to suppress her needs to accommodate others.

A woman caught in the feminine trap has learned to suppress and deny her own needs, putting other people's needs ahead of her own. She will practically do somersaults, rearranging her schedule to accommodate everyone else. She is unable to say no to many demands made of her even if she is overwhelmed with obligations. She will not hesitate to put her own needs for sleep, recreation, or leisure last when she perceives that someone needs her: in some cases, she may not even be aware that she *has* needs for recreation and leisure.

The good girl is so sensitive to the approval of others that she is afraid she will be seen as selfish if she refuses to put others first. She feels guilty because she herself also feels that it is selfish to think of herself and put herself ahead of others. "Selfishness" has many negative connotations in our culture because it implies callousness and self-absorption. A "healthy selfishness," however, is essential to our well-being. It is a form of self-love and means taking care of ourselves to enable us to better nurture others. We need to put our needs first so that we have the emotional energy to cope with the many demands placed on us. If we do not nurture ourselves, we are prone to become tired, ill, and burnt-out, and then we are of no use to anyone. We must take care of our needs. If we do not, who will?

In this chapter, we have outlined some ways that women can satisfy their need to be loved by men without denying their natural urges. We have discussed methods of breaking free from the self-defeating "good girl" behaviors. First of all, we can challenge and liberate ourselves from the impossible standards applied to our weight just as our predecessors freed themselves from their rigid sexual constraints. We should become aware of the craziness inherent in the conflicting messages we receive daily and the absurdity of trying to conform to these messages. We need to make our own rules instead of following the arbitrary standards set out for us by Madison Avenue. Secondly, we have to challenge the myth that thinness brings eternal love and happiness and to detach slimness from the many emotional connotations we have placed on it. Thirdly, we should examine the numerous psychological, physical, and financial costs of our obsession with thinness. It is certainly not worth dying for! Fourthly, we can learn to like and accept our bodies as they are instead of trying to remold them to fit the current fashion. We need to recognize that no matter what we do, certain aspects of our bodies will not change. It is time to make the body a friend instead of an enemy. Learning to think "healthy" instead of "thin" is another way that we can break free from our destructive patterns. In addition, we should recognize that in our efforts to be loved by men, we are packaging ourselves as products instead of persons, as good girls instead of adult women. Lastly, we need to develop a "healthy selfishness." We have to accept our needs for affiliation and bonding and learn to nourish ourselves emotionally as a first step in meeting these needs. We can learn to satisfy our emotional needs directly instead of making food our lover. We can stop denying ourselves and go after our *just* desserts!

Chapter 12

Toward a New Consciousness

Together, women can help create a world where each of us lives with respect in our body whatever our size. It is a goal that deserves our full attention.

—Pat Lyons, *Fitness, Feminism and the Health of Fat Women*

In the preceding chapter, we described some individual strategies that women can use to liberate themselves from the tyranny of slimness. However, it is difficult to make many of these changes in a society where eating without guilt and being fat are seen negatively. The cultural pressures are so overwhelming that it is hard for us to fight this battle alone. No matter how much we strive to feel comfortable with food, with our weight, and with our bodies, we still need societal support for these changes. The first step is for us to raise our consciousness about the cultural myths about thinness, fatness, and body size that we have swallowed hook, line, and sinker. We need to examine these myths critically rather than accept them unquestionably. We also have to become aware of our own prejudices against women who do not meet the current standards of bodily perfection. We must acknowledge our own biases and associations towards fat. Secondly, we should fight both personal and legally sanctioned forms of discrimination against women who deviate from the "ideal" weight. Thirdly, we ought to provide new opportunities for women of all sizes to feel good about themselves and their bodies. Lastly, we should join together to create new images, new role models, and a new vocabulary to replace the current one.

FAT IS JUST A SIZE

In the past, the myth was that there were two kinds of girls — "good" girls and "bad" girls, with no gradations in between.

The current mythology is that there are only two types of women—"thin" or "fat." Thin women are good, moral, beautiful, healthy, happy, and in control of their lives. Fat women are bad, ugly, disgusting, physically unfit, lazy, and lacking will power. There is an overwhelming dichotomy in people's minds so that one is either thin or fat, with no vocabulary to describe the women who weighs somewhere between 110 and 210 pounds. The truth is that most of us fall somewhere in between the model-slim covergirl and the morbidly obese woman. Yet we have accepted this way of thinking and will call ourselves "fat" (i.e., "bad") when we are really "normal" in terms of what women should look like. Since the word fat has come to have such derogatory connotations, the average-sized woman feels bad and worthless because she can only place herself in the "fat" (i.e., "bad") category.

Inherent in the thin-fat dichotomy is the myth that fat is unattractive, unhealthy, a sign of pathology, and an indication of moral weakness. This prejudice is so strong that when we ascribe this term to ourselves, it generates self-hate and loathing. It is important to point out that fat is not universally seen as ugly, and antifat attitudes are limited primarily to affluent Western nations. Many cultures see rounded, ample figures as highly sexual and full-bodied women with large hips and flesh on their bodies as beautiful and erotic. The obsession with thinness is only a recent phenomenon and is the prototype of a fad (Rothblum, 1989). Viewed in this light, fat is not inherently unattractive but only a reflection of what is "in" in today's culture.

Another component of this myth is that only thin people are healthy. Rothblum (1989) disputes the myth that obesity is necessarily related to poor health. The truth is that fat people can be and often are as healthy as non-fat people, and it is only at *both* extremes of the weight spectrum that weight constitutes a serious problem. Many of the studies on the effects of weight on health do not have adequate controls, and it may very well be that it is the *dieting* as much as the extra weight that contributes to the high blood pressure and other problems experienced by heavy people. While it may be true that there are problems associated with being heavy, we need to weigh these against the physical and psychological problems resulting from the constant dieting and the persistent isolation and depression over being fat. The health hazards of starving the body and depriving it of nutrients can be so much more pronounced than the physical problems that may ensue from being twenty to thirty pounds over the current norm. As Hilde Bruch, one of the foremost authorities on eating disorders states:

> In spite of the handicaps of obesity, the most damaging of which are culturally created, to react with overeating in the face of conflicts and difficulties is relatively harmless. It is less destructive personally and less of a social liability than many other abnormal reactions in the face of similar stress, such as hypertension, suicide, neurotic or psychotic breakdown, alcoholism or, in recent years, amphetamine or other drug abuse. (Bruch, 1973, p. 386)

Not only are fat people supposed to be physically unhealthy, they are also psychologically unhealthy and neurotic, according to the myth. "If she is fat, there must be something wrong with her," or so the reasoning goes. In fact, fat people are no more or no less emotionally healthy than thin people, and being fat does not necessarily make one immature, unstable, maladjusted, or any of the hundreds of labels we give to fat people. When fat persons do experience depression and anxiety, it is often in response to societal ostracism rather than a sign of internal psychopathology.

Finally, fat people are viewed as morally weak, lazy, and lacking in will power. Such an attitude is so acceptable that even the national magazine *Newsweek* allowed Ken Hecht's blatantly bigoted article ("Oh, Come on Fatties!" MY TURN, Sept. 3, 1990) to be printed. Hecht castigates those who have not lost weight as successfully as he has and essentially views them as weak-willed individuals who are just too lazy, unmotivated, and undisciplined to take off their extra pounds. The causes for being fat are complex and multifaceted. Whereas some people can successfully shed pounds and keep them off through diet and exercise, others cannot because of biological factors and/or lowered metabolism due to constant dieting. In addition, many people simply *do not care* to put in that kind of effort to lose a few pounds, just as many people do not care to put in so much work to learn a foreign language. Oh, sure, maybe they could *if they really wanted to*, but does that make them weak, lazy, and morally inferior if they do not? If they are healthy and content with their bodies, why should they be made to feel as though there is something wrong with them for not continually dieting and trying to lose weight?

We have to learn to see fat as just a size and detach it from all of its pejorative connotations. Women come in all shapes, colors, and sizes. Just as we need to separate thinness from all of its excess meanings, we must examine the myths about fat and learn to see the big body as just one variation of the many different human sizes and shapes.[2]

Examining the myths and misconceptions about weight can be a first step in helping us study our own biases and starting to correct them. Rothblum and Brown (1989) state that there need not be any shame in this. She goes on to say that just as white North American women learn to be sexist, racist, and homophobic, almost all of them also learn to hate and fear fatness, especially in themselves. It is difficult to grow up in this society without being exposed to the "thin is beautiful" concept and its counterpart that "fat is ugly." Thus, no matter how progressive and unbiased we like to think of ourselves, most of us have internalized societal anti-fat biases. We can pay attention to our spoken and unspoken thoughts. What do we say to ourselves when we see a fat woman heaping her plate and going for second helpings? What do we think when we see a fat person in a bikini or wearing clothes that expose rather than hide her body? How often do we compliment people on their looks when they have lost weight? As we start to pay attention to our own thoughts and actions, we have taken a first step in understanding fat discrimination.

FIGHTING FAT DISCRIMINATION

There exist both personal and legally sanctioned forms of discrimination against fat people. Marcia Millman, in her book *Such A Pretty*

---

2. For a comprehensive treatment on the subject of fat oppression, the reader is referred to *Overcoming Fear of Fat* (1989) edited by Esther Rothblum and Laura Brown (New York: Harrington Park Press.)

Face (1980), poignantly describes the daily humiliations suffered by the fat person in America. She illustrates the daily stigmatization and abuse that fat people, particularly women, go through simply because of their size. She notes that even if obesity is unhealthy, people with other health problems are not condemned in the same way. In addition to the overt forms of teasing, taunting, and fat-bashing that are displaced onto fat children and adults, there are some subtle, unwritten rules for fat people—that they should not buy nice clothes, that they should always be trying to lose weight, that they should not expect relationships with the opposite sex, and that they should postpone living until they are thin.

The discrimination manifests itself in other ways as well, in that products are not designed with the large woman in mind. Fat women face daily worries and increased isolation because seats in airplanes, restaurants, and moviehouses are not constructed for fat people. Similarly clothes are not designed with them in mind. Why should a large woman forgo designer clothes and restrict herself to loose-fitting sacks? Why should she be excluded from going to movies, travelling in comfort, or dressing in style? The very exclusion of these amenities for the fat woman tells her that there is no place for her in this society, that she should hide in shame and not show herself in public.

In addition to these subtle and not so subtle messages, there are also legally sanctioned fat discrimination practices. Airline companies are notorious for overt discrimination practices against weight gain, and demand that their female employees be routinely weighed. These women risk losing their jobs if they weigh in above the artificially created standards of body weight. Whereas some of this is done under the benevolent guise of "health," what these companies are doing is fostering an epidemic of eating disorders—anorexia, bulimia, and the like.

A recent case involved the firing of an airline stewardess for having had the audacity to put on about twenty pounds in about as many years! The stewardess, a former beauty queen in her twenties, was now in her forties. She was attractive, healthy, and competent in her twenties and attractive, healthy, and *more* competent in her forties, having had many years of experience behind her. She could perform her job as well and probably far better than many of her younger, less-experienced colleagues—yet she was being fired simply because she did not meet weight standards and could not lose the weight as fast as the airlines demanded. Although the fat discrimination was rationalized on the grounds of health concerns—that the stewardess could not perform her job due to health reasons—there was nothing to suggest that this was the case. The stewardess would not be considered obese or even fat by most people's standards. She had only gained twenty or thirty pounds at most—yet she was being discriminated against in the most blatant fashion simply for looking like most women her age. What would happen if we stopped hiring pilots with receding hairlines? This is not too different from the newscaster who was let go because she stopped looking like a model. Both women sued.

It is important for us to actively band together and fight these glaringly unfair employment practices. We can call attention to these types of discrimination, and we can also refuse to be a party to them. We can fight fat oppression on both a personal and political level. We need to stop marketing products and services to women which are clearly not in their self-interest and are only geared to make money. A blatant example of this is the practice of liposuctions on slim women. We were shocked to hear of a surgeon who recently performed an abdominoplasty on a young woman—a very slim woman—*after* she told him that she was in treatment for anorexia and bulimia! This is just as shocking as a recent newspaper article describing the use of liposuctions and breast implants for adolescent girls, some as young as age 13. We need to call attention to and stop these practices when they clearly do not have the best interests of women in mind.

CREATING NEW RESOURCES FOR FAT WOMEN

Not only must we fight oppression against fat women, we need to actively provide opportunities for the fat woman to feel good about herself. It is clear that not every woman, can, wants to, or should lose weight. What can those women do who, regardless of their best efforts, remain a large size? Are they doomed to a lifetime of hiding? How can a woman feel good about herself in spite of the strong anti-fat societal attitudes? If a woman with only a little cellulite on her hips and tummy can feel hideous, what is the very fat woman to do? How can she learn to feel powerful and worthy? How can she move from shame to self-esteem? Is it truly possible to do so, we may ask. The answer is yes. This section focuses on some strategies for the very fat woman, the woman who despite repeated efforts to lose weight, remains fat, whether due to genetic reasons, set point, or any other number of factors beyond her control.

F.A.T. (Fat Acceptance Therapy) is a non-dieting group approach to physical wellness, insight, and self-acceptance (Tenzer, 1989). Through group support and understanding, the fat woman can share her pain with others and start to become angry at the fat oppression instead of feeling that there is something inherently wrong with her. She learns to understand her body and reclaim it. She finds ways to deal with and cope with social disapproval and stops hiding. She starts to listen to her body and its needs: rather than continuously dieting, she eats in a reasonable manner and in response to hunger. She begins to honor and love her body instead of disowning it. The strategies of Fat Acceptance Therapy can be applied, of course, for any woman who does not fit the "ideal" body norm, but they are particularly needed for the fat woman. As Tenzer states:

> In order to be free from conflict, a person must find acceptance or change. For 95 percent of the 30 million American women who wear size 16 or larger (NAAFA, Inc., 1987), dramatic weight change is not possible. Therefore, the best alternative is fat acceptance. I am grateful I found that. (p. 47)

Another resource for the fat woman is the Ample Opportunity (AO) organization whose aim is to create a social environment accepting of all body sizes and to assure access to a high quality of life for the fat woman. Nancy Barron and Barbara Hollingsworth Lear (1989) began the organization in Portland, Oregon in 1984. Ample Opportunity sponsors physical activities, workshops, and information sharing which promote physical and emotional well-being for fat women. Activities have included fat awareness gatherings, support groups, and a monthly newsletter to help women explore misconceptions about fat and learn ways of coping with anti-fat attitudes. In addition, physical activities such as swims, belly-dancing, rafting, and canoe trips promote physical health and body acceptance. Community education and combating prejudice are also goals of the organization. The philosophy of Ample Opportunity is that all members of society will benefit from greater size acceptance and that fat women need not lose weight in order to live a full, healthy life. The AO motto states, ''A good life is the best revenge.'' Although most of the women in AO have been over the average weight of the general population, average weight women have also joined some of the activities. Organizations like AO can help all women feel good about their bodies. Unfortunately, this sort of organization is not available in most geographical areas. We need to create similar opportunities in other areas as well.

Women do not need to live in Portland, Oregon to find support and acceptance in liking their bodies. The National Association to Aid Fat Americans (NAAFA) has chapters nationwide. In addition, magazines such as *Radiance: The Magazine for Large Women* and *BBW* (Big Beautiful Woman) can provide ongoing support for thousands of fat women.

Great Shape: The First Exercise Guide For Large Women (Lyons and Burgard, 1988) is another publication geared to helping the fat woman feel good about her body. Pat Lyons (1989) describes how, as a fat woman all her life, she learned to turn self-hatred into self-love through movement and sports. Lyons combines principles of sports psychology and feminism to help women use sport and dance as ways of nourishing their bodies and empowering themselves. Because fat women are so embarrassed to bare their bodies, they have avoided exercise classes where they might be exposed to ridicule. Lyons states that deprivation of movement leads to being cut off from the body, and that nobody is meant to live from the chin up. Sport and exercise can help women re-own their bodies and feel fit and powerful. She wrote her book so that fat women like herself could benefit from her experience. She writes: ''Finally, I'd found my answer. I, Pat Lyons, a fat woman, could live my life in peace. I could be healthy and fit, but I'd always be fat. And being fat was finally O.K. I had a right to respect the body I was born to have, and no one had a right to ridicule or humiliate me anymore'' (p. 71).

CREATING NEW IMAGES, NEW ROLE MODELS AND A NEW VOCABULARY

Since we derive so many of our ideas of what is good and beautiful from the images that daily bombard us, it makes sense that if we are to start changing the way we feel about our bodies, we need new images of what is beautiful. We are reminded of the 20-year-old daughter of one of our acquaintances who was obsessed with slimness and who, like millions of other young women her age, saw herself as unattractive and ugly because she did not have the ideal body type. She went to the Middle East for a year, and in that short time, she changed the way she saw herself. She felt good about her large hips and no longer was obsessed about slimming down nor contemplated surgical interventions. Why? Is it possible that living in a culture where reedlike bodies are not idealized, where eating is viewed as a normal activity, and where the daily images of what is beautiful ranges across a wide variety of body types, could have made the difference?

Another example concerns a dance troupe from Argentina that was making a world tour. We watched the dancers as they beautifully danced the tango and moved smoothly, gracefully, and sensually across the stage. What stood out for us was not so much the beauty of the dance but the fact that none of these dancers had slim bodies, and many were fat—yes, fat—with protruding stomachs, full hips, and even flab. It would be inconceivable to see dancers with such ''imperfect'' figures accepted in this country. Yet these performers appeared very relaxed and at ease with their bodies. They moved gracefully, and it was obvious they perceived themselves as beautiful and sexy. Clearly, the obsession with slimness is not universal. Other cultures do not view only thin bodies as beautiful, and their stars are not all model-thin. We need to depict a larger variety of body shapes and body types in our commercials, television sitcoms, and movies. The fat or average weight person does not need to be restricted to "character" roles. Having more shows like *Roseanne* or *Babes*, a television sitcom about three overweight sisters, is a start in the right direction. Maybe the day will come when these shows will not be described as shows about overweight people but shows about people, without making an issue about their weight. Even more important may be allowing women who do not fall on either extreme of the weight continuum—women who are neither skinny nor fat, women whose bodies may follow the natural contours of age and pregnancies, women with sagging breasts and rounded tummies, woman of all body types and shapes—to be depicted as attractive and sexy. Seeing role models with less than perfect bodies can liberate us from constantly attempting to adhere to a body type that may be impossible to attain.

In addition to new role images and new role models, we need a new vocabulary to describe women who do not fall under the category "thin." The term "fat" has very negative connotations, and its synonyms also elicit negative reactions. We have found over twenty words synonymous with a large size, e.g., heavy, corpulent, full-bodied, large, big, plump, stout, hefty, rotund, chubby, chunky, overweight, stocky, hippy, busty, roly-poly, tubby, paunchy, flabby, ample, bulky, rounded, and "zoftig." Some of these words are less emotionally charged than others, but very few are neutral. There are also very few words to describe the medium-sized woman. As we pointed out before, since we only have variations of thin and fat, the woman who does not fall in the thin category views herself as fat and therefore bad, weak, and unattractive. With the sexual revolution, we freed ourselves from the "good girl"—"bad girl" dichotomy and the negative connotations associated with sexual appetites. We need to end the "thin-fat" dichotomous thinking and stop giving size arbitrary meaning.

ONWARD TO THE 1990s

Before the 1960s, society told us what we could and could not do with our bodies. We were told to deny our sexuality so that men would love us. With the sexual revolution, we reclaimed our bodies and started expressing our sexuality. Society is again telling us what we can and cannot do with our bodies. We are told to repress our oral appetites and stay thin so that men will love us. We need to liberate ourselves from these shackles just as our sisters liberated themselves from the tyranny of sexual oppression. We must join together to create a new consciousness. It is our fervent hope that in the 1990s women can free themselves from the imprisonment of their own and society's making. We hope that we can re-examine our values and reject some of the "junk" that we have been feeding ourselves.

It is time for a new revolution.

References

Adams, C. (1955). "Making marriage work." *Ladies' Home Journal*, July, p. 28.

American Psychiatric Association. (1980). *Diagnostic and Statistical Manual of Mental Disorders*. (3rd ed.). Washington, DC: Author.

Baber, A. (1987). "Men." *Playboy*. March, p. 32.

Banner, L. W. (1983). *American Beauty*. Chicago: University of Chicago Press.

Barbach, L. (1975). *For Yourself: The Fulfillment of Female Sexuality*. New York: Doubleday.

Barron, N. & Lear, B. H. (1989). Ample opportunity for fat women. In L. Brown & E. Rothblum (Eds.). *Overcoming Fear of Fat* (pp. 79-92). New York: Harrington Park Press.

Bell, R. M. (1985). *Holy Anorexia*. Chicago: University of Chicago Press.

Blotnick, S. (1985). *Otherwise Engaged: The Private Lives of Successful Career Women*. New York: Facts on File.

Boston Women's Health Book Collective. (1971). *Our Bodies, Ourselves: A Book By and For Women*. New York: Simon & Schuster.

Botwin, C. (1985). *Is There Sex After Marriage?* Boston: Little, Brown.

Brown, H. G. (1962). *Sex and the Single Girl*. New York: Pocket Books.

Brown, L. (1985). Women, weight, and power: Feminist theoretical and therapeutic issues. *Women & Therapy*. 4(1), pp. 61-71.

Brown, L. (1989). Fat-oppressive attitudes and the feminist therapist: Directions for change. In E. Rothblum & L. Brown (Eds.). *Overcoming Fear of Fat* (pp. 19-30). New York: Harrington Park Press.

Bruch, H. (1973). *Eating Disorders: Obesity, Anorexia Nervosa and the Person Within*. New York: Basic Books.

Carliss, R. (1982). "The new ideal of beauty." *Time*, August 30, pp. 72-77.

Cash, T.F., Winstead, B. A., & Janda, L. H. (1986). "The great American shape-up." *Psychology Today*, April, 20(4), pp. 30-37.

Cassell, C. (1984). *Swept Away: Why Women Fear Their Own Sexuality.* New York: Simon & Schuster.

Chartham, R. (1987). *The Sensuous Couple.* New York: Ballantine.

Chernin, K. (1981). *The Obsession: Reflections on the Tyranny of Slenderness.* New York: Harper & Row.

Chodorow, N. (1978). *The Reproduction of Mothering.* Berkeley: University of California Press.

Comfort, A. (1972). *The Joy of Sex.* New York: Crown.

Corlat, I. H. (1921). "Sex and Hunger." *Psychoanalyst Rev. 8.* 375.

Cross, A. W. (1985). "Diahann Carroll." *Shape*, November, 5(3), pp. 89-90; 108-109.

Dodson, B. (1974). *Liberating Orgasm.* New York: Body Sex Designs.

Dowling, C. (1981). *The Cinderella Complex.* New York: Simon & Schuster, Pocket Books.

Eisler, B. (1986). *Private Lives.* New York: Franklin Watts.

Ellis, A. & Abarbanel, A. (Eds.) (1973). *The Encyclopedia of Sexual Behavior.* New York: Jason Aronson, Inc.

Enos, C. & Enos, S. F. (1986). "The secret life of the American woman." *Ladies' Home Journal*, February, pp. 101-103; 172-175.

Farb, P. & Armelagos, G. (1980). *Consuming Passions: The Anthropology of Eating.* New York: Washington Square Press, Pocket Books.

Fezler, W. & Field, E. S. (1985). *The Good Girl Syndrome.* New York: Macmillan.

Freedman, R. (1986). *Beauty Bound.* Lexington, MA: D. C. Heath & Co.

Freudenberger, H. & North, G. (1985). *Women's Burnout.* New York: Doubleday.

Friday, N. (1973). *My Secret Garden.* New York: Simon & Schuster, Pocket Books.

Friday, N. (1975). *Forbidden Flowers.* New York: Simon & Schuster, Pocket Books.

Friedan, B. (1962). *The Feminine Mystique.* New York: Dell.

Garner, D. M., Garfinkel, P. E., Schwartz, D., & Thompson, M. (1980). "Cultural expectations of thinness in women." *Psychological Reports, 47,* pp. 483-491.

Gay, P. (1984). *The Bourgeois Experience: Victoria to Freud. Vol. I: Education of the Senses.* New York: Oxford University Press.

Gilligan, C. (1982). *In a Different Voice.* Cambridge, MA: Harvard University Press.

Haire, G. S. (1940). *Encyclopedia of Sexual Knowledge.* New York: Eugenics Publishing Co.

Hall, G. S. (1904). *Adolescence.* New York: D. Appleton.

Halmi, K. A., Falk, J. R., & Schwartz, E. (1981). "Binge eating and vomiting: A survey of a college population." *Psychological Medicine, 11,* pp. 697-706.

Hardman, R. K. & Gardner, D. J. (1986). "Sexual Anorexia: A look at inhibited sexual desire." *Journal of Sex Education and Therapy. 12 (1),* 55-59.

Hawkins, II, R. C. & Clement, P. F. (1984). Binge eating: Measurement problems and a conceptual model. In R. C. Hawkins, II, Fremouw, W. J., & Clement, P.F. (Eds.), *The Binge-Purge Syndrome.* (pp. 229-251). New York: Springer.

Hecht, K. (1990). "Oh, come on fatties!" *Newsweek,* September 3.

Hite, S. (1976). *The Hite Report.* New York: Macmillan.

"J." (1971). *The Sensuous Woman.* New York: Dell.

Jong, E. (1973). *Fear of Flying.* New York: Signet.

Jong, E. (1984). *Parachutes and Kisses.* New York: Signet.

Kantrowitz, B., Witherspoon, D., Williams, E. & King, P. (1986). "Too Late for Prince Charming?" *Newsweek,* June 2, pp. 54-58.

Kaplan, H. S. (1979). *Disorders of Sexual Desire.* New York: Simon & Schuster.

Katzman, M. A., Wolchik, S. A. & Braver, S. L. (1984). "The prevalence of frequent binge eating and bulimia in a nonclinical college sample." *International Journal of Eating Disorders, 3,* pp. 53-62.

Kennelly, A. (1955). "Don't go, Olaf," *Ladies Home Journal,* July, p. 52.

Kinsey, A. C., Pomeroy, W. B., Martin, C. E. & Gebhard, P. M. (1953). *Sexual Behavior in the Human Female.* Philadelphia: W. B. Saunders Co.

Kirkendall, L. (1977-78). "A new bill of sexual rights and responsibilities." In *Focus: Human Sexuality,* pp. 7-9.

Lagemann, J. K. (1954). "Romance can ruin your marriage." *Cosmopolitan,* March, pp. 60-63.

Landers, A. (1985). "What 100,000 women told Ann Landers." *Reader's Digest,* August, pp. 44-46.

Lasch, C. (1979). *The Culture of Narcissism.* New York: Warner.

Levin, E. (1986). "The new look in old maids." *People,* March 31, pp. 28-33.

Levine-Shneidman, C. & Levine, K. (1985). *Too Smart for Her Own Good?* New York: Doubleday.

Lowe, C. (1988). "Sweet surrender: Sugar's not the bad guy you think it is." *Self,* December, pp. 134-136.

Lyons, P. (1989). Fitness, feminism and the health of fat women. In L. Brown & E. Rothblum (Eds.). *Overcoming Fear of Fat.* New York: Harrington Park Press.

Lyons, P. & Burgard, D. (1988). *Great Shape: The First Exercise Guide for Large Women.* New York: William Morrow.

"M." (1972). *The Sensuous Man.* New York: Dell.

Mademoiselle. "Make your body bare-able." June 1985, p. 24.

Mademoiselle. "Legs are back! Can you bare them?" June 1985, pp. 172-175.

Marks, S. (1988). "How I lost 80 pounds." *Woman's Day,* September 13, pp. 54-69.

Marshall, M. (1984). *The Cost of Loving.* New York: G. P. Putnam's Sons.

Masters, W. H. & Johnson, V. E., (1966). *Human Sexual Response.* Boston: Little, Brown.

Masters, W. H., Johnson, V.E., & Kolodny, R. C. (1982). *Masters and Johnson on Sex and Human Loving.* Boston: Little, Brown.

Millman, M. (1980). *Such a Pretty Face.* New York: Norton.

Money, J. (1985). *The Destroying Angel.* Buffalo, NY: Prometheus Books.

Moody, F. (1985). "Love after 30." *L. A. Weekly,* June 21-27, pp. 21-39.

Moscovitz, J. (1986). *The Rice Diet Report: How I Lost Up to 12 Pounds a Week on the World-Famous Weight-Loss Plan.* New York: Putnam Publishing.

Myer, L. (1982). My mother's prayer. In Roth, G. *Feeding the Hungry Heart* (pp. 164-165). New York: Signet.

Norman, D. C. (1955). "100 pounds off..." *Ladies' Home Journal*, July, pp. 54-55; 84-85.

Norwood, R. (1985). *Women Who Love Too Much.* Los Angeles: Jeremy P. Tarcher.

Offit, A. K. (1981). *Night Thoughts: Reflections of a Sex Therapist.* New York: Congdon & Lattes.

Ondercin, B. A. (1979). "Compulsive eating in college women." *Journal of College Student Personnel, 20,* pp. 153-157.

Orbach, S. (1978). *Fat Is a Feminist Issue.* New York: Paddington.

Phoenix Gazette. (1985). "25% of women try food binges," November 7, p. C-6.

Phoenix Gazette. (1990) "Better than sex cake," September 19, p. FD-2.

Rechtschaffen, J. S. & Carola, R. (1980). *Dr. Rechtschaffen's Diet for Lifetime Weight Control and Better Health.* New York: Ballantine.

Reichman, S. J. (1977). *Great Big Beautiful Doll.* New York: E. P. Dutton.

Rueben, D. (1970). *Everything You Always Wanted To Know About Sex* But Were Afraid To Ask.* Boston: Bantam.

Rombauer, J. & Becker, M. (1975). *The Joy of Cooking.* New York: New American Library.

Rossner, J. (1983). *August.* New York: Warner.

Roth, G. (1982). *Feeding the Hungry Heart.* New York: Signet.

Roth, G. (1984). *Breaking Free From Compulsive Eating.* New York: Signet.

Rothblum, E. D. (1989). "Women and weight: Fad and fiction." *The Journal of Psychology, 124*(1), pp. 5-24.

Rothblum, E. & Brown, L. (Eds.) (1989). *Overcoming Fear of Fat.* New York: Harrington Park Press.

Russell, R. (1984). "Quotable quotes." *Reader's Digest,* July, p. 137.

Russianoff, P. (1982). *Why Do I Think I Am Nothing Without A Man?* New York: Bantam.

Sadowsky, P. (1985). "Food: the 'bad' and the beautiful." *Cosmopolitan,* November, pp. 416-417.

Shaevitz, M. H. (1984). *The Superwoman Syndrome*. New York: Warner.

Shulman, A. (1969). *Memoirs of an Ex-Prom Queen*. New York: Alfred A. Knopf.

Stout, M. (1986). "Hot chocolate." *Vanity Fair*, February, p. 65.

Taylor, R. B., DeLong, W. B. & Freisinger, M. (1985). "Don't just sit there—fit tips for desk workers." *Shape*, November, *5*(3), pp. 50-55.

Tenzer, S. (1989). Fat acceptance therapy (F.A.T.): A non-dieting group approach to physical wellness, insight, and self-acceptance. In E. Rothblum & L. Brown (Eds.). *Overcoming Fear of Fat*. New York: Harrington Park Press.

Thompson, C. (1985). "Faith can help take fat off." *Phoenix Gazette*, November 16.

Weldon, F. (1981). *The Life and Loves of a She-Devil*. New York: Ballantine.

Williams, M. (1958). "The well-fed bridegroom." *Ladies' Home Journal*, April, p. 122.

Woodiwiss, K. (1974). *The Wolf and the Dove*. New York: Avon.

Wouk, H. (1955). *Marjorie Morningstar*. Garden City, NY: Doubleday.

Wurtman, J. J. (1984). *The Carbohydrate Craver's Diet*. New York: Ballantine.

Index